A Parent's G

Please return/renew this item
by the last date shown.
Books may also be renewed by
phone and Internet.

Other parenting books from Continuum

Getting Your Little Darlings to Behave – Sue Cowley
Help your Teenager Succeed at School – Michael Papworth
Educating your Child at Home – Jane Lowe and Alan Thomas

A Parent's Guide to Primary School

How to get the best out of your
child's education

Katy Byrne and Harvey McGavin

continuum
LONDON • NEW YORK

Continuum

15 East 26th Street	The Tower Building
New York	11 York Road
NY 10010	London
	SE1 7NX

British Library Cataloguing-in-Publication Data
A catalogue record for this book is available from the British Library.

ISBN: 08264 7379 2 (paperback)
Typeset by Fakenham Photosetting Limited, Fakenham, Norfolk
Printed and bound in Great Britain by Hobbs the Printers

Contents

1   The Education System   1

2   Pre-school Education   9

3   Choosing a School   13

4   Your Relationship with the School   27

5   What your Child Learns   42

6   How your Child Learns   59

7   A Child's Eye View   79

8   The Teacher's Perspective   99

9   Special Needs   110

10   School Life   127

11   Getting Ready for Secondary School   141

Resources   152

Index   157

For Joe and Luke

'Education is not the filling of a pail, but the lighting of a fire.'
WB Yeats

Acknowledgement

Thanks to all the people who agreed to be interviewed for this book, and especially to Fou Fou Savitsky, Anna Turvey and Rachel James for their comments.

Introduction

There are literally hundreds of books on childcare, covering every aspect of how to look after your children. But when the big day arrives and they start school, it's easy to hand them over to the teachers, and think no more about it.

We drop them off at 9am and pick them up at 3.15pm – but what do they do all day? This book aims to guide you through the primary school years – what your child learns, how they learn it, the ways in which you as a parent can help your child and how to deal with the complexities of school life

ONE

The Education System

What goes on inside schools has changed significantly in the last generation. Even if you are a young parent, the education your child is embarking on will be very different from the one you received.

Out of all the public services, education has been subject to the most reforms in recent years. Generally, there has been a trend towards increased bureaucracy. The introduction of the National Curriculum, SATs, Ofsted inspections and countless new initiatives and schemes has increased the paperwork that teachers and schools have to deal with. It is a common complaint of teachers that they spend less and less time actually teaching and more and more time filling in forms and marking.

This has influenced the way children are taught today. A teacher has less freedom to explore topics at leisure, there are fewer diversions, and what matters is covering the curriculum. With such a heavily prescribed curriculum, critics say there is not as much room for creativity. The advantages of having an education system that is the most tested and inspected in history is that standards – especially in primary schools – can be shown to be improving.

In England and Wales, children must attend school (or be schooled) between the ages of 5 and 16 and compulsory education is divided into primary and secondary stages. Primary education up to the age of 11 was formally established by the 1944 Education Act: prior to this, children had been taught in elementary schools up to the age of 14.

I

After the age of 16, there is further education (colleges accessible to anyone over the school leaving age) and higher education or universities. A generation ago, only ten per cent of children went on to university, but the government has set itself the target of 50 per cent of school leavers going on to higher education by 2010.

While a child's education will, on average, now finish later, it is also starting earlier. Children are legally required to start going to school at the start of the term after their fifth birthday, but in practice when they start will vary from area to area. The trend is for children to start school younger than this. Most schools now admit new pupils into their reception class at only one point in the year, although occasionally they may have a double intake (usually in September and January) to introduce younger children slightly later.

In practice, most schools admit children who are going to turn five at some point during the coming school year, meaning that the youngest will start school just after their fourth birthday. The pros and cons of starting school young will be looked at in a later chapter. And while the school leaving age has been the subject of plenty of debate and many law changes over the years (being changed from 12 years at the turn of the last century to 14 in 1918, 15 in 1944 and 16 in 1970) the school starting age has not, until recently, attracted quite so much attention.

How old does a child have to be to start school? At what age should a child be expected to sit quietly and still for extended periods, hold a pen in their hand and begin to draw letters and numbers? Some educational thinkers believe that a five-year-old child is not physically ready for such tasks.

In Britain, the age at which children start formal education is creeping downwards. Pre-school facilities have improved and become more regimented under the government's Early Years strategy, which promises nursery places for all four-year-olds who want them. Some local education authorities have Early Years Centres, a kind of combined nursery and playgroup in a school setting that takes children from the age of eighteen months up to the age of five. Many schools have nurseries attached that take children for the year before they officially start school. It is worth noting, however, that admission to the nursery does not guarantee a place at the school.

The year in which children officially start school – the year they turn five – is called reception. Their progress through school is now referred to in numbered years, so what used to be called the first year is now Year 1, going up to Year 6 (the last year of primary education) and then Year 11 (GCSEs) and Year 13 (A levels) in secondary schools. It can be difficult at first to remember the year that corresponds to a child's age – if in doubt, add five to the year number and you'll get the approximate age of the children in it.

These years are grouped into key stages, so that at primary level children go through Key Stage 1 (5–7 years) and Key Stage 2 (7–11 years), which correspond to infants and juniors. Secondary education covers Key Stages 3 and 4.

In some areas a three-tier system of first, middle and high schools persists, whereby children leave primary school at 8–9 years and go into a middle school where they stay until they start secondary education at 12 or 13 years. Most of these areas – which include Suffolk, Northumberland, Wiltshire and the Isle of Wight – are phasing out the three school system, mainly because it does not fit easily with the requirements of the National Curriculum.

The National Curriculum, and most of the defining features of the British education system, were introduced as a result of the Education Reform Act of 1988, the biggest recent piece of legislation affecting schools. This also established:

- the local management of schools
- league tables and testing
- grant maintained schools
- new rules on collective worship and RE.

The Department for Education and Skills (DfES) is the government department responsible for education. It has been through several incarnations, and was known as the Department of Education and Science in the 1980s, and the Department for Education and Employment in the 1990s, reflecting the changing priorities of the times.

Today, the main jobs of the DfES are:

- the control and administration of national education policy
- to finance the education system, mainly through local

3

education authorities (LEAs), though some types of school are funded directly

■ to set and monitor standards in education via Ofsted, the schools inspectorate.

The government's education policy is delivered by local education authorities. These are part of local councils (and therefore democratically accountable) and they are responsible for early years education (pre-school), schools, education and youth services. They vary greatly in size – one LEA may be responsible for 50 schools while another may have 500 in its area – and in the quality of education they provide. Even neighbouring LEAs in similar circumstances can produce wildly differing results.

The main responsibilities of an LEA are:

■ to administer government policy

■ to distribute funding for the schools from the money allocated by central government

■ to plan the educational provision according to local needs – LEAs decide on the closure and merger of existing schools and the building of new ones

■ to make sure that there are fair school admissions policies

■ to provide services to meet the needs of individual children (for example, pupils with Special Educational Needs or children off school for medical reasons)

■ to monitor school attendance in their area

■ to set local standards for schools and monitor their performance – LEA draws up an action plan when a school goes into 'special measures' because it is failing its pupils.

OFSTED

The Office for Standards in Education (Ofsted) was set up in 1992 with the aim of improving the quality and standards of education and childcare through independent inspections. It also provides advice to the Secretary of State and produces reports on various aspects of the education system's performance. Prior to this, local authorities were responsible for inspecting their own schools, a state of affairs that resulted in some very patchy quality control of educational provision.

Ofsted's primary function is to manage the regular inspection (every 6 years) of the 24,000 state schools in England, although it also reviews the performance of LEAs and inspects teacher training courses. Since 2001 its role has included the inspection of childcare providers, including registered childminders.

The other major public bodies concerned with education in England are the Qualifications and Curriculum Authority (QCA) and the Teacher Training Agency (TTA).

The QCA, established in 1997, is responsible for maintaining and developing the National Curriculum and for the regulation of all public examinations. Since 1994, the Teacher Training Agency has been in charge of overseeing the general supply and training of schoolteachers and trying to attract people to the profession through advertising.

The education systems of Scotland, Wales and Northern Ireland are broadly compatible with that of England, but there are also many differences. All children in the UK start school around the age of 5 (a little earlier in Northern Ireland) and slightly adapted versions of the National Curriculum apply in Wales and Northern Ireland, although not in Scotland.

Wales is the closest to the English system, although it has its own inspectorate, ESTYN, and around a third of primary schools have Welsh as their sole or main language of instruction.

The Education and Training Inspectorate have the job of inspecting schools in Northern Ireland where, despite efforts at integration, most schools are still segregated along religious lines. Northern Ireland has also retained many of its grammar schools, and a small number of primary school children have subsidized places in their prep schools.

The system in Scotland has always been completely separate to the rest of the UK. The curriculum is decided by local authorities and headteachers and is much less strictly prescribed than the National Curriculum. The Scottish Executive Education Department recommends that 80 per cent of a school's time should be spent on the core subjects of the 5–14 programme – language, maths, expressive arts, environmental studies and religious, moral, personal and social education – and it is left up to the school to decide how to spend the remaining 20 per cent of the time.

The school

State primary education in the UK is free and schools are not allowed to select children according to their ability. Schools in the UK have to be open for 190 days a year, generally from September to July.

School terms

Nearly all schools work to a traditional pattern of three terms, just as they have done for more than a hundred years. But lately, another tradition has been added to this familiar scenario. Every year, usually around the start of the summer holidays, as parents are juggling work and childcare arrangements and complaining about how holiday companies push up their prices during the long summer break, articles start appearing in the newspapers proposing the abolition of the three-term school year in favour of something more practical. Reformers argue it's a centuries-old system, arranged around religious festivals and harvest times and which has no place in a secular, post-industrial society. Children get worn out by long terms and then forget what they have learnt during the long summer holidays – something proved by research.

But teachers and their unions generally oppose change, saying they don't want to lose the long summer holidays which are one of the perks of the job and provide some 'down time' to recover from the strains of school life. Introducing piecemeal changes would disrupt family life even more, they say.

Some schools, notably secondary city technology colleges, have already made the change, introducing a five-term year of eight-week blocks separated by two-week holidays with no half terms and four weeks off in the summer. Now the Local Government Association, which represents councils, is recommending a six-term year consisting of two seven-week terms before Xmas and four six-week terms afterwards. These would be regularly spaced, regardless of when Easter falls, with alternate one- and two-week breaks (with a couple of days extra holiday in October) and five weeks off in the summer. The LGA hopes the plan will take effect from September 2005, standardizing the school year and seriously diminishing one of the most enduring and popular features of school life – the six-week summer holiday.

The term dates and the way their weekly timetable is arranged is up to individual schools, but they must by law provide a minimum of 21 hours teaching in Key Stage 1 and 23.5 hours in Key Stage 2.

The government has pledged that class sizes in England's primary schools should not exceed 30 – in the rest of the UK they are significantly lower than that. Usually, one teacher will take a class of one year group although in small, rural schools classes can be mixed age groups, which might result in some children staying with the same teacher for more than a year.

Faith schools

Today, nearly 800,000 children are educated in Church of England primary schools and just over 400,000 in Catholic schools, together accounting for around 40 per cent of all children.

In 1998 the Islamia primary school in Brent became the first Muslim school to join the state sector. There are also Methodist, Jewish and Sikh faith schools. The present Labour government is in favour of creating more faith schools and the Church of England currently has plans for another 100 schools.

Faith schools within the state sector are under the control of the LEA and have to teach the National Curriculum, and to all intents and purposes are the same as state schools. Where they differ is in their admission policy. This varies from school to school, but proof of adherence to the faith in question is usually necessary, although some schools reserve a percentage of their intake for non-believers.

Independent schools

Around six per cent of primary age children are educated independently. If they could afford it, many more parents say they would pay for their child to be educated independently – more than 60 per cent according to a survey that was, admittedly, commissioned by the Independent Schools Information Service.

Private (or independent) schools receive no public funds: some are privately owned and run for profit while others will be funded by a charitable foundation. Most independent schools teach the same subjects as a state school, although they may also offer Latin or other subjects which have disappeared from most state schools. Pupils take the same tests at GCSE and A level but independent schools do not have to teach to the National Curriculum, nor do they have to comply with education targets. Pupils at independent primary schools, usually called preparatory schools, don't generally take SATs, for example. Instead, the preparation hinted at in their title refers to the Common Entrance examination. As pupils approach the age of 11 (or 13), more and more time is devoted to studying for the Common Entrance Exam – the hurdle that needs to be cleared to get into many independent secondary schools.

TWO

Pre-school Education

Most children experience some sort of childcare before they start school – more than half of all women with dependent children under the age of 5 go out to work. The government would like more women to get back into work after having children and recognize that the lack of affordable and suitable childcare is a major problem. In social policy the government recognizes that good quality pre-school education and services are vital in areas of deprivation. So in 1998 it announced a National Childcare Strategy. This promised all four-year-olds access to a free, part-time nursery place. By April 2004 all three-year-olds who wanted free, part-time education would have it. Currently, around 79 per cent of three-year-olds receive a free place.

These places are provided in the private, voluntary and maintained sectors, in community playgroups, in nursery schools and classes and also with registered childminders. If your child is in full-time care or at a very expensive nursery then the government will pay up to the value of a part-time place, and you pay the rest.

Formal childcare falls into the following categories:

1. State Nursery Schools.
   - Are open similar hours to schools for older children but take children from the age of three or four. Offer full- or part-time places.
   - Must have at least one qualified teacher and one qualified nursery assistant for every 20 children.

2. Nursery classes in state primary schools
   - Usually take children from the age of three or four and operate during school hours and terms.
   - Normally offer five half-day sessions a week, although some offer full school hours.
   - Must have at least one qualified teacher and one qualified nursery assistant for every 26 children.

3. Private nursery schools
   - Take children between the ages of two and five and offer full- or part-time places.
   - May act as feeders to independent primary schools.
   - Must have at least one qualified teacher for every 20 children.

4. Day nurseries/creches
   - Look after children between 0–5 years for the whole working day or according to parental needs.
   - Are usually run by local authorities or voluntary organizations
   - Must have at least one adult for every eight children and at least half the staff must have a qualification recognized by the local authority.

5. Childminders
   - Look after children of any age – pre-school, or school age after school hours and in the school holidays.
   - Must be registered with the local authority, which decides how many children they can look after.
   - Usually look after children in their own home.

6. Playgroups or Pre-schools
   - Are usually community groups run on a not-for-profit basis.
   - Charge around £3–£6 for a three-hour session, with the parents often expected to help.
   - Are sometimes only open for a few sessions a week.

Ofsted regulates and inspects childcare for all children under 8. The only providers of childcare that are not registered or inspected are nannies and au-pairs.

The type of childcare or pre-school education you choose will depend on various factors such as distance to your home or place of work, availability of places, cost and the hours you need.

With programmes like Sure Start, which aims to bring a range of health and education services to families with children under four, and the Neighbourhood Nurseries Initiative, which will fund 900 affordable new nurseries in deprived areas, the government is placing a lot of emphasis on good pre-school education. Research shows that:

- Children have a better start at primary school if they have already attended some kind of pre-school or nursery.

- State-run nurseries often give a better start as they place more emphasis on learning through play than private nurseries, which use more didactic teaching.

- Any kind of pre-school is better than none, especially for children from disadvantaged families.

- The risk of anti-social behaviour can be reduced by high-quality pre-school care.

- Full-time attendance gives no increased benefits over part-time.

- Nursery schools and classes attached to schools give the best quality care.

- The higher the qualifications of the staff, the better the intellectual and social development of the children.

In government-funded nursery schools or classes Education Acts apply, covering inspections, what children are taught and the staff's training and qualifications. Nursery schools and classes are covered by the Foundation Stage, which is the first stage of the National Curriculum and covers children aged 3–5. It has six Early Learning Goals which the nursery school or class will be working towards. These are:

- Personal, social and emotional development – includes behaviour and self-control, sense of community and making relationships.

- Communication, language and literature – includes linking sounds and letters and reading, writing and handwriting.

- Mathematical development – includes calculating and shape, space and measures.

11

- Knowledge and Understanding of the World – includes cultures and beliefs and exploration and investigation.
- Physical development – includes health and bodily awareness and using tools and equipment.
- Creative development – includes music, imagination and exploring different materials.

Learning through play

The role of play in education has been emphasized by psychologists since the beginning of the century, and the benefits of learning through play are now well established. Play gives children many learning opportunities, including:

- Acting out and making sense of real-life situations
- Exploring, investigating and experimenting
- Inhabiting many different situations
- Collaborating with others
- Expressing ideas and feelings confidently
- Developing an awareness of themselves and others.

Many nurseries will say that they practice learning through play, but staff have to be aware of this philosophy. Learning through play is not simply putting children in a room full of toys. The role of the adult who is present is vital. He or she models appropriate behaviour, asks the children questions and stimulates conversations. In this way play can motivate children, help develop their memory and concentration skills and contribute to their emotional, social and cognitive development.

Learning through play is about using appropriate language. So, for example, if a child is playing with a red car you might say, 'Oh that's a lovely red car. Can you get it to go faster or slower?' Introduce the right vocabulary and the child will pick up those little things through playing and they will learn without feeling pressured, grasping what you are trying to tell them.

Sharmaine, mother of Denika, 12, and Kiana, 9.

THREE

Choosing a School

Choosing a school for your child used to be a straight-forward matter – most people simply sent their children to the school nearest their house. These days it's an altogether trickier business.

Love them or hate them, league tables have shown that there are wide disparities in schools' performances. As parents we are more informed about schools than ever before – how they do academically, which subjects they perform best and worst in and also what their social make-up is. We know how many children have free school dinners, how many have special educational needs, and what proportion have English as a second language.

League tables have become a kind of pop chart of primary education. The good schools' names go up in lights every time newspapers publish the annual top ten, the underperforming schools all get named and shamed at the other end of the tables, and the vast majority of schools, which are well run and where children learn happily, are made to look average.

There's a lot more information available to parents – in Ofsted reports and league tables – to help you choose. And there's a lot more choice – you are allowed to send your children to schools outside your local area if you want to.

All this information adds to our anxiety about making the choice. This idea of 'parental choice' is a relatively new one. The 1988 Education Act gave parents the right to 'choose' a school that had spare places. Until then, the LEA decided which schools they should keep going by controlling admissions to keep viable numbers in those schools. The 1988 Act basically changed the meaning of 'full' from 'up to LEA admission limit' to 'what the buildings will actually contain'.

This has meant that schools operate in a competitive environment, and because parents want the best for their children, the pressure on places in high performing schools has become intense. In reality, 'parental choice' only means that you have the right to express a choice: it doesn't mean you will get what you want if you choose an 'oversubscribed' school where the number of applications exceeds the number of places.

In this situation schools have more choice than parents over the children they admit. The most commonly used criteria are where you live, whether you have any other children already at the school and, in the case of faith schools, religious observance. Some heavily oversubscribed schools even have to employ the services of a professional surveyor with a measuring wheel to decide which children get a place. The distance between your front door and the pavement, or the positioning of a road crossing, just might make a difference. If you are lying about your address you should be aware that the Local Education Authority can verify this with a home visit. So this is not really advisable.

The main thing to remember when starting to look at schools is that the one that appears to be the best school may not necessarily be right for your child. There are a variety of factors that help you make the decision and, unless you are really unlucky in where you live, there should be more than one school where your child will learn happily.

We had absolutely no idea about schools when we moved into the area – when you are just married you don't even think that far ahead. And then we began to hear that there was a good school just around the corner and we thought, 'Oh, that's lucky'.

We went and saw the school on a music hall evening and the experience of sitting on those tiny little chairs – being six foot five it was like *Gulliver's Travels* – actually brought back a flood of memories of my own childhood and thinking, 'Oh yes, I remember this is what school's like – it's not so bad', particularly at that age.

Jamie, school governor and father of Isobel, 11, Anna, 5, and Maisie, 4.

What is a catchment area?

The catchment area of a school is not fixed – it expands or contracts from year to year depending on the number of children applying to the school and where they live. It can be defined as the area around the school within which, in a given year, children will get a place in the school. So for one year the catchment area of a popular school might reach a mile from the school, if there are simply not that many children trying to get in that particular year. Another year it may only extend to a few streets away if, for example, a greater proportion of places are going to siblings of children already in the school who may live miles away.

Be realistic about the catchment area when you are thinking of schools. If you live a long way outside the approximate catchment area of a school then in years gone by it may not have been worth applying. Some schools like to be placed as a parent's first preference, so if you put an unrealistic choice as your number one this may harm your chances of getting into another good school that likes to be put as a first preference.

What makes a good school is subjective. For some parents it is all about academic achievement. Others may value great sports facilities, a good reputation for music or art, or good transport links over excellent SAT results. Whatever your immediate priorities, keep thinking flexibly and try to take in the whole picture. Think about what you are looking for in a school. This may include considerations such as:

- Distance from home. Do you really want to be part of the school run or is it important to be within walking distance of the school. If you would be using public transport what is the journey like? How much will it cost? Is it likely to tire your child out?

- Friends. Will your child know anyone at the school? Is that a good thing or a bad thing? Your child may need the security of going to a school with other friends, or you might look on it as a chance to make new friends.

■ Is your child particularly bright or talented in one area? Is there a school that has strengths in that subject? Does your child have any Special Educational Needs (see later chapter)? Which school is best equipped to meet them?

■ Are there any non-educational aspects of school life that particularly matter to you? Do you hate the idea of a strict uniform policy? Is religious ethos important? Do you prefer schools that have plenty of outside space?

Find out as much as you can about all the schools near you. You may already have a school in mind, but just because it is your school of choice does not mean they will offer your child a place. You need to find out about all the likely schools in your area. These are your best sources of information:

1. The School. Each school produces a prospectus every year. As well as lots of glossy photos of happy, studious pupils, it contains information about admissions policy, the most recent Ofsted report and what the school sees as its strengths. But what the prospectus leaves out can be as important as what it puts in. There should be other documents available from the school such as its home-school agreement, governor's report, religious education syllabus and behaviour policy. If the prospectus raises any questions, write them down so you can ask them if you decide to visit the school.

2. The LEA. Local education authorities produce booklets detailing all the schools in its area and how to apply to them. If languages other than English are commonly spoken in the area then translated texts should also be available. This type of information is often distributed through playschemes or local doctors' surgeries and local libraries.

3. School league tables. Every year the Department for Education and Skills (DfES) publishes performance tables for primary and secondary schools. They don't give a complete picture of the school, but they do provide a guide as to how well the school is doing. League tables have been criticized for being a simplistic measure of school performance. To give a fuller picture, the

government has introduced the concept of 'value added', which takes into account a school's circumstances.

4. Ofsted reports. While school league tables give a snapshot of school life, the Ofsted report provides a much more detailed account. All Ofsted reports are available on the net from *www.ofsted.gov.uk*. When looking at them it is important to view them in context. Is the school getting better or worse? Has the headteacher changed since then (a good headteacher is widely recognized as one of the most significant factors in school success)? What does it say about the atmosphere of the school?

5. Local parents who have had children at the school. Remember, what they say is very subjective. What may be right for their child may not be right for yours.

There is really only one way to find out what you feel about a school, and that is to go and see it for yourself. By the time you get to this stage you probably know which school or schools you favour, but that could all change with an actual visit to the school. At primary schools you may be taken round by the headteacher or deputy head (secondary schools often have 'open days' with pupil-led tours), which is your chance to ask all the questions you want to and find out about the school's ethos. You can take your child along with you, depending on his age, but you may be less distracted if you leave him at home. It could also cause problems if your child sets his heart on a school that he may not get into or that is your last choice. Things to remember:

- Use your ears and eyes. Do the children seem happy? Are the staff harassed? Is there a relaxed atmosphere between the children, teachers and support staff?
- What does the school sound like? Is it quiet, contented and studious or noisy, hyped-up and stressed-out?
- Are the children busily absorbed in their work or do they seem bored, as if waiting for something to happen?
- It can be useful to visit at the beginning or end of the school day. Do the parents, children and staff hang around to chat or are they all desperate to get home?
- Remember to make a note of any questions you have and

don't be afraid to ask them. Schools are used to closer scrutiny from parents these days, so you need not feel like a pushy parent. If they are uncomfortable with questioning this tells you something about the school.

■ Is the library well-stocked and well-used? What are the computer facilities like?

■ Is the children's work displayed with pride on the walls or is it curling at the edges and looking like it has been up there for years?

■ Find out if there is an active Parent-Teachers' Association. This is usually a sign of a good school. How does the school communicate with the parents? Is there a notice-board for parents, a regular newsletter or a website?

■ There may be specific things you want to find out about, like the arrangements for school dinners, uniforms, sports, and so on. Don't be afraid to ask.

There was a school in our street. We went round to look at it and I thought it had a really nice atmosphere. The headteacher was obviously completely committed and knew all the kids' names. It just had a really warm feeling and the artwork was just all really impressive. And there was a convenience factor in that it was on our street and another factor was that a friend of ours was going to send her daughter there and had checked it all out. I thought if she was happy to send her daughter there then it would be alright for Imogen. So we didn't look at any other schools.

Louise, mother of Imogen, 6.

How to read league tables

Primary school league tables compare performance, expressed as the percentage of children achieving level 4 and above in their Key Stage 2 SATs tests in English, Maths and Science. They also include background information on the school – for example, the type of school it is, the number of pupils it has, their age range and the number and percentage of children who have special needs and statements.

The average SATs scores locally and nationally (which in 2003 was 234 out of 300) are also provided for the sake of comparison. Newspapers publish lists of the schools that have the most improved overall point score – often showing dramatic improvements in the space of a few years. In 2003, Wellington Primary School in Tower Hamlets, London, came top, scoring 279 – up from 83 in three years.

When the league tables for primary schools were first published in 1996, they were criticized for not providing an adequate assessment of the school's circumstances. For example, a school may not appear to be doing well but could be working wonders with an intake which includes a high proportion of children with English as a second language or with special needs. On the other hand, well-resourced schools with middle-class intakes are sometimes guilty of 'coasting'.

In order to more accurately reflect a school's achievements, the government has developed a 'value added' measure. This looks at individual pupils' Key Stage 1 results, works out what they could be expected to achieve at Key Stage 2, compares their actual results with those of other pupils at the same level and produces an overall figure for the 'value added' by the teaching at the school. A value added measure of 100 is average, meaning pupils have made the progress expected of them. Anything above 100 means they have exceeded expectations, while a figure below 100 means they have made less progress.

Although the variations in value added figures might seem quite small they do reveal large differences in performances. Any school scoring above 102 is in the top five per cent of schools nationally, while those achieving less than 98 are in the bottom five per cent. The top value added school in 2003, Delaval Community Primary School in Newcastle upon Tyne, scored 105.5.

Applying to primary schools

Once you have chosen your favourite school you must make sure you apply in time, using the right procedure and in the way that will give your child the best chance of getting in. Remember that your child may not get into your first choice, so try not to set your heart on it. Keep an open mind about other schools. Schools can be strong in some areas and weak in others – the perfect school does not really exist. Apply to your local school even if it is not your first choice: if you don't get into your other choices, your best chance on appeal may be at the school nearest to you.

Timing your application

You need to be thinking about schools by the time your child reaches his third birthday, as many schools have started to admit 4-year-olds. Although legally your child does not have to start school until the term of his fifth birthday, realistically he may not be able to get in if you want him to start a year later than the rest of his peers.

More and more schools are opening nurseries for children aged 3–4. These usually only offer a morning or afternoon session, although they sometimes build up to a full day. But bear in mind that you will have to apply separately for a place at the school and that having a place at the nursery does not guarantee you one. Make sure you know when the closing date for applications is – most schools and LEAs are pretty strict about this and will not normally consider late applications.

Admissions bodies

At the risk of stating the obvious, you do have to apply to a school to get your child into one. Do not assume that he will somehow be automatically allocated a place at your nearest primary school. The LEA is legally obliged to educate your child, but if you don't apply your child will be allocated a school only after all those who did apply have found places.

The method of applying varies from area to area and from school to school. The admissions body to which you apply can be the school itself (usually the case for faith and other

20

selective schools) or the LEA (for most other state schools). The school will be able to tell you which is the case.

School admissions handled by the school

If the school handles its own admissions then they will be able to supply you with an application form and tell you the closing date for applications. In faith schools the admissions policy is determined by the governors, although in some cases (mostly with Church of England schools) the LEA is involved and the school is its own admissions authority.

From the September 2004 intake, faith schools have been banned from interviewing pupils to assess their religious knowledge and commitment following criticism that schools were using these as a means of academic selection by the back door. However, you will almost certainly still need to demonstrate your adherence to the faith in some other way – for example, regular church attendance – so find out in good time if a letter from your local priest or religious leader is required to support your application.

School admissions handled by the LEA

If you want your child to go to a school for which the LEA has responsibility (most state primaries) then you must fill in a LEA admissions form stating your preferred choice of school. Usually you will be asked to give a second choice too. Some schools prefer to be put as first choice, so it is important to be realistic about your options at this stage and to do a bit of research on the catchment area. Each LEA has an admissions team that can advise you as to whether you have any chance of getting into an oversubscribed school or not. But don't waste a 'first choice' on a school you realistically haven't a hope of getting into.

At present, you fill in a different form for each school, but from 2005 LEAs will coordinate school admissions (and in some areas they already do this). This means that you will fill in a single form with your order of preference and then send it off to the LEA. If you qualify for more than one school then you will be offered the school you ranked highest on the list.

All parents within the LEA will then find out on the same day which place their child has been allocated. This is to eliminate, as far as possible, a situation where parents receive multiple offers of school places, which can lead to delays and confusion over allocations.

There may be things relevant to your application that you will have to support with letters from either a doctor or a social worker who knows your child. For example, a child with recurring arthritis may need a school within easy walking distance of home, or if a sibling is at a special school far away you may prefer a school en route to make getting them both to school more easy.

How admissions work

School and LEA admissions policies vary and details will be outlined in the LEA booklet mentioned above and in the school prospectus. Lots of schools have enough places for the children that apply, but many popular schools receive far more applications than they have places. When this happens they will have clearly stated rules deciding who gets a place. These 'oversubscription criteria' – and the order in which they apply – will be printed in the LEA booklet and should be readily available from the school. Usually they include:

- The sibling rule – usually the first in will be those with siblings at the school.
- Catchment area – those living nearest to the school will be next.
- Feeder schools – for secondary school admissions, these are primary schools that traditionally send pupils there.
- Medical or social reasons why your child should go to the school – these will have to be backed up by letters from doctors or other professionals.
- Church attendance – for faith schools only, when this will often be the first rule.

If your application is unsuccessful

If your child does not get into the school of your choice you will be informed by letter. This will also tell you that you have the right of appeal, how to do it and when the deadline for appeal is. Sometimes this is worded in such a way as to suggest that any appeal would be useless. While it is true that most appeals are lost this is not always the case, and if you feel that you do have grounds then you must make a written appeal.

When they said she didn't have a place my whole life, you know, dropped like a stone. Then when I applied for the school and they refused it again all I did was cry. I met a parent in McDonalds and she put me in touch with another parent and they helped me out and told me how to appeal which we did successfully.

If I had not met that parent I would be really struggling. The letter they sent me turning me down was really putting me off appealing. They are not encouraging you at all to appeal, they say you don't have a chance to appeal. It's more difficult for me as English is my second language. Because when they write a letter there are some words they use that I don't understand. They said there is no guarantee that she will get in. It makes me feel down, you know.

Nadia, mother of Jamal, 7.

Since government legislation came into force restricting infant class sizes to 30, parents are finding it more and more difficult to win appeals. In 2000/01, 35 per cent of parents who appealed won their case, a one in three success rate but somewhat less than in previous years – in 1995/96 the figure was 48 per cent. This does not mean it isn't worth appealing, but be realistic about your chances of winning and explore other options.

In most cases an independent appeals panel will hear the case put by the admissions authority explaining why you were not offered a place. In the case of voluntary-aided schools (faith schools), the body to which to appeal would normally be the governors of the school. If the panel decides the admissions authority did not give sufficient reason for refusing your application then they will go on to hear your side – why you want your child to go to that particular school and why you think he should be offered a place. You should mention any factors that you think are relevant. The appeals panel then weighs up whether they think the benefits to your child of going to that particular school are outweighed by the negative impact of that school having another pupil in the class.

If the panel upholds your appeal then the school must take your child. If not, you need to consider your other options. You could ask to go on the waiting list for the school, as places do sometimes come up after the start of the school year. But remember that you can move down waiting lists if parents whose children fit the admissions criteria better than your child apply.

There are different rules if a place was refused because an infant class (up to age 7) had reached its legal limit of 30. In that case the appeals panel will only look at two things:

1. Did the admissions authority stick to its own rules in your child's case? If it did not then your child will win the appeal. If it followed its rules to the letter then the appeal fails.

2. Did the admissions authority act 'unreasonably', that is, was its decision not based on the facts of the case?

If you are not happy about the way the appeal was conducted, then you can take it up with the local government ombudsman.

Changing schools

If, for whatever reason, you are applying for a place in a school mid-year, find out from the LEA whether to apply via them or to the school directly. If the school tells you it is full it is still worth applying and, if you are turned down, appealing. Despite the limit of 30 on infant class numbers, you may still be offered a place in a full class if there is no other suitable school within a reasonable distance.

Excluded pupils

If your child has been excluded from a school, you still have the right to apply for any other school you like. A previous exclusion cannot by itself be a reason for turning down an application, but if your child has been permanently excluded from two schools and the last one was within the last two years then the school has a right to turn his application down. In this case you have no right of appeal. If your child has displayed challenging behaviour in previous schools but

24

has not clocked up two permanent exclusions with one in the last two years, then the school can turn him down for that reason but in this case you do have the right of appeal.

For more information about what to do if your child is excluded contact The Advisory Centre for Education *(www.ace-ed.org.uk)*, which will give you detailed advice about what your rights are and how to challenge exclusions. Their contact details are at the back of the book.

Starting school

He went from a very play-oriented, few-rules nursery environment to a highly-structured school with a lot of rules and it was a shock. What he found absolutely crucifying in those first two weeks was the playground. What a horrible scary place.

Socially he felt on his own and miserable and he didn't know what to do with himself without friends to hold on to. He had accidents because he was too scared to ask where the loo was and he didn't know where it was. He felt bewildered by the size of the environment because it was so much bigger than his nurseries – big halls, big dining tables and things like that.

Choosing his food, too; he's never had any choice about his food in his entire life and he's then presented with a canteen situation. He had no idea what to do – it was a completely new situation for him.

Julia, trainee teacher and mother of Daniel, 6, and Jasper, 4.

Starting school is a big deal for children and for some of them it is not an easy transition. Many schools ease children in gently with a week of half-day sessions and followed by the full week. Others throw them in at the deep end with full days from the beginning. Whichever is the case, expect your child to be very tired in the first few weeks of school. Don't pack their time after school with play dates or extra activities. Here are some other tips to make the start of school easier:

- Try and make prior contact with other children starting the school. Seeing a familiar face in the playground on the first day will be a big help.
- Talk to your child about going to school. Walk past the school and show them where the children go in, where they have their classes and where the playground is.
- Try to get them used to spending periods of time away from you.
- Find out the name of their teacher, if possible, and talk about him or her.
- Try on the uniform, if there is one and they want to do it.
- If your child is nervous about school, don't force the subject on them.

The reception class of most schools is very much play based, but children will adapt to school much more easily if they are already able to do certain things. These include:

- Sharing and taking turns.
- Going to the toilet by themselves and being able to wash and dry their hands properly.
- Dressing and undressing mostly unaided, including coats and shoes.
- Sitting still.
- Concentrating for short periods of time for book reading.
- Understanding simple instructions.
- Knowing how to ask for things politely.
- Knowing how to use a knife, fork and spoon.
- Recognizing his own name.
- Tidying away toys.

FOUR

Your Relationship with the School

I'm just really keen to know what Louis is doing in school. Before he started school he was at a nursery in the mornings and I spent all afternoon with him. Then he started in the reception class and suddenly he was at school all day. From the outset I just found that really strange, not knowing what he was doing from 9 to 3. He doesn't give me much feedback so my only way of knowing what he is doing all day is from his teacher.

Tricia, mother of Louis, 7.

Developing a good relationship with the school will not only satisfy your curiosity about what your child is doing all day – it will also aid your child's education. Research has shown the positive effects parental involvement can have in developing numeracy and literacy skills. Establishing good lines of communication with your child's school and regularly exchanging information with her teacher can only help your child's progress through the school.

The information you have to offer might seem trivial, but don't underestimate the important contribution a simple remark can make. Mentioning that your child is not keen on her new shoes so an admiring comment would be appreciated can help ease the troubled mind of your youngster. Be sure to communicate more serious news, such as a family illness or

27

bereavement. All information helps the teacher – and through the teacher the school – build a picture of your child and her life outside the school.

There can be barriers to parent/school communication, such as language and culture, but it is in everyone's interest that these are overcome. Your child's school and the people in it are going to be part of your life for years to come, so it is up to you to make the relationship work.

For your child, as well as for you, school can be an intimidating place at first. If you are comfortable in the school environment some of that feeling will pass on to him or her. Children spend around 15,000 hours at school in their primary years. Although they are not in your care while they are there, your responsibility for how they spend that time there does not end at the school gates. You can only find out about what they are doing and how it is all going if you are informed and involved.

Your attitude

You might remember what it was like to start primary school and your impressions of a place which would become as familiar to you as your own home. The novelty of putting on the uniform, the strangeness of the buildings, the sea of new faces and the excitement of having your own desk and chair and your first impressions of a place which would become as familiar as your own home. Sports days, assemblies, the fighting and the friendships, lessons outside in the summer and frosty playgrounds in winter ... all these memories are jogged when your own child begins primary school.

We might not have realized it at the time, but our primary school years are important – they are the foundations on which our whole school career rests. In these years a child's attitudes to all sorts of things – authority, peers, even learning itself – are formed. Different factors come into play when a child goes into secondary school; the power of hormones can change the sweetest 11-year-old into a nightmare on teen street. But generally if a child has enjoyed primary school and been stimulated and inspired by her teachers then there is no better start to a successful school career. On the other hand, if she learns to fail at primary school then she may repeat the pattern at secondary level.

I've seen some parents who've probably had a very stressful time themselves at school who are really quite anxious about coming into school. I always make sure I'm there in the playground before the school day starts and when the school day finishes, because it's really difficult for some parents to phone up and make an appointment to come and see me or to go to the office but they might be able to come up and grab me in the playground.

Schools do understand that there are issues about adult literacy as well. Don't be afraid as a parent, if you can't read and write, to say to the school 'I can't do that', or if you've had difficulties at school the school will be really understanding about that.

Kate, deputy headteacher and mother of Eliza, 6.

It is hard to underestimate the role of school in shaping the people we are today. Maybe they truly were the happiest days of your life. Perhaps you were captain of the sports team, top of the class and rose to be head boy, developing leadership skills you used to great effect in your career. Maybe you went to a school where you called the teachers by their first names and studied in an informal atmosphere or were you nurtured in a small rural school where you formed a close bond with fellow pupils?

Maybe you spent your whole school life on detention and the teachers always seemed to be on your back as you struggled with the work. Maybe you were in the bottom stream and associate school with failure. You may have gone to an enormous school and felt your face was lost in the crowd. Were you frightened by school and intimidated by its size or the demands it made on you? Did everyone copy your innovations to the uniform and want to be your friend or were you the one circling the playground, never fitting in?

To some extent, these early experiences have shaped your life, just as they will shape your child's life. They also influence the way you view your child's school.

One of the main things that a school represents is authority. School is the first major institution to challenge your role as a parent, teacher and carer. Managing that loss of control can be difficult, especially if you have been at home looking after an only child and so – without the distraction of a younger brother or sister to care for – starting school can suddenly leave a big gap in your day. And if your own schooling was one long running battle with teachers, littered with detentions and other punishments, you might resent handing over your child to the care of people who represent your former tormentors.

It can be a good idea to take time to reflect on your school life: how you felt about the teachers and the work. Overall, do you have positive or negative feelings? Whatever the case, it is important to recognize that your own experience of school shapes your attitude and that you could be passing those attitudes on without even realizing it.

This chapter is aimed at helping you to communicate with the school, particularly if you have problems with school. Schools are much more open, welcoming environments than they were 20 years ago (and you are that bit older!), so parents should aim to have an equal relationship with the people in them.

Getting involved

I didn't know what to expect when Denika started school, but I've got better over the years. When she first started I would go in there and they did encourage me to mill around and look around, and I did that but I wasn't involved as much as I should have been. But after a year or two I got stuck in there and started helping. I think support is important – I've learned that along the years.

Sharmaine, mother of Denika, 12, and Kiana, 9.

One of the first things you can do when your child starts school is to introduce yourself to their teacher. Teachers are busy people so do not attempt to corner them for a lengthy explanation of your child's eating habits, but an initial introduction helps them match parent with child.

Some schools have highly organized induction weeks where children start part-time and parents are allowed to come in for an hour or two to ease their introduction to school life. At other schools, children attend full time from the start, which can be hard for the summer babies. But nearly all schools will arrange for a brief meeting with your child's teacher at the very beginning of the year.

30

Getting involved with the school immediately opens channels of communication. When your child begins school full time, your responsibilities as a parent do not diminish, at least as far as the school is concerned. Nearly all successful schools rely on parental involvement as one of the main factors behind their continued success. Parents at some schools can make a full-time job out of fundraising and organizing the many events that make up the modern school calendar.

Extended schools

During the day, schools are hectic places, full of hundreds of kids and dozens of teachers and staff engaged in the business of teaching and learning. Then suddenly, come half past three, they are all but empty and the sports facilities, IT equipment and library are locked up for the night.

Certain schools, notably community schools, have tried to make their premises more accessible to local people, realizing that it can foster a sense of involvement as well as getting the most use out of equipment that lies idle for large parts of the day, and for weeks at a time during the holidays.

A lot depends on having a sympathetic caretaker and a headteacher who doesn't mind sharing the school with people other than its pupils. The government is keen to encourage more schools to do so and has announced it is to set up a new breed of school – the extended school.

The extended school is nothing to do with building more classrooms, it is about welcoming more people onto the premises. By 2006, 240 extended schools will be established under a £52 million pilot scheme, and there will be at least one in every LEA. These will combine a school's education function alongside other open-all-hours community services such as health centres, creches, libraries, internet cafes and even police stations and post offices.

It is not an entirely new idea – a network of village colleges was set up in Cambridgeshire by the county's then education chief Henry Morris in 1920s to bring together 'all the various, vital but isolated activities in village life'. If the scheme is successful, schools should take their rightful place at the heart of the local community.

Starting to get involved in the life of the school can feel like being a guest at a party where you don't know anyone. If this is the case, then it's time to brush up on the underestimated skill of small talk. It is a bit like starting a new job – it makes life a lot easier if you try to get on with everyone.

If you find the whole playground social scene a bit stressful, you are probably not alone. Having children forces you to meet other people with children. Some of them will become lifelong buddies, others you may not be able to stand. Julie may be your daughter's best friend, but that does not mean you will automatically get on with Julie's mum and dad. But remember, you don't actually have to. All you have to do is keep on friendly speaking terms in order to arrange a bit of after-school play.

To begin with it was daunting being one of the men in the playground. I remember times when I took him to things like playgroup, and going in and seeing all these women I just thought 'I do not want to go in there, this is not for me'. You do feel alien, but to be quite frank if you forget your hang-ups it can be the most beautiful and fun experience you could ever have. I mean you don't even see the gender barriers because as soon as you open up they just break down and there is nothing there any more.

Rodney, father of Jesil, 6, and Elai, 3.

A good school creates a feeling of community and is a supportive environment for your child to grow up in. Getting involved in the school helps both your child and the school feel like you care. You may care very much about your child's education, but simply be unable to spare the time – it is estimated that the parents of one in four children work full time and getting time off work for school events can be difficult. If this is the case, schools will often accept another family member or carer in your place, so long as they are told about it in advance.

> It would be nice to be involved more in the school. But I've got two children, I'm a single mother and the things they do in the evening often start at 7.30 so all I can do is help make some of the food when they have a party. It would be good for me but it's difficult at the moment because I cannot leave my children.
>
> Mila, mother of Andrew, 15, and Abigail, 6.

In primary schools, particularly in the early years, when children have not yet embarked on the serious business of SATs and homework, activities such as baking, craftwork or simply reading offer an opportunity to contribute to school life, depending on where your skills lie. If you don't feel comfortable performing in front of 30 curious 7-year-olds, then don't be put off, there are other things you can do, like decorating the hall for a special event or offering to drive the school minibus. Talk to other parents or people who work at the school (often parents themselves). They can be an invaluable source of information about what is going on at the school and how things are managed.

The first thing to do is to let your child's teacher know you are interested in becoming involved. They will be happy to suggest things for you to do. If the staff can match other faces and people to your child then your child simply makes more of an impact. Filling in the background of your child's life helps the teacher to put their behaviour, likes and dislikes into context.

> I remember a friend of mine who's a teacher saying to me, 'You've got to make your child known to the teacher'. Otherwise, she said, they are just this anonymous person in the class. There is this big group of children in the middle of every class that do okay. They don't shine out because they are really bright or get singled out because they are either naughty or need extra help. She said this is a real problem area because these children in the middle don't get enough attention. I think Louis is in that group so I feel I have to work extra hard to make the teacher realize who he is.
>
> Tricia, mother of Louis, 7.

Parents' evenings

If your idea of a parents' evening is listening to a lengthy discourse on how wonderful your child is, then think again. A few minutes of quality time and the chance to ask a quick question or two is a more realistic expectation. But the parents' evening is the main chance you get to have an uninterrupted chat with your child's teacher, so make the most of it – and be prepared:

- Be punctual – a ten-minute time limit is typical, and latecomers mess up the schedule.
- Talk to your child beforehand. Tell her you are going to talk to her teacher and see if there is anything she wants you to ask.
- Make a short list of questions or issues you want to discuss.
- Cover the most important points first in case you run out of time.
- Try to identify areas where your child may benefit from extra help at home.
- Let the teacher know of things, however trivial, that bother your child about school.
- Give the teacher feedback, and if you think she is doing a good job, thank her for it.

After the meeting tell your child about the things that were discussed. This gives her the message that you and her teacher care about her progress and are working together to support and help her do her best. If the teacher has given negative feedback try to couch it in more positive terms: 'She thinks your spelling could improve if we practised together at home', or 'She knows you can do better at . . .', etc. Nobody likes to think they are being talked about behind their back, so be open with your child about what was discussed.

Parent teacher associations

I think people look at the PTA and think, 'Oh, posh women'. They feel intimidated. It's almost like a little club, although it's not trying to be. We're trying to open up this 'school as part of the community' idea, but in fact it ends up being a little clique of parents who do everything. I actually find it really helpful because if I've got any doubts about something I can usually approach somebody in the PTA and they will know what to do.

Tricia, mother of Louis, 7.

In the not too distant past, parents were actively discouraged from getting too involved in school life. But changes in legislation and social habits have seen parents welcomed into the school fold.

Parent Teacher Associations are a great way of getting to know teachers and other parents. There are 12,500 PTAs in the UK, each one providing an invaluable line of communication between parents and schools. Their function and make-up varies, but the main aim of a PTA is to foster better communication between parents and teachers. Their role includes:

■ Fundraising to provide 'extras' for the pupils
■ Organizing social events for parents and children
■ Providing helpers for outings and special events
■ Running clubs for sports, music and drama
■ Keeping parents informed about education issues.

Ideally, the school listens to the parents' concerns and harnesses every ounce of support they can from parents. For their part, the parents learn more about the school and how to support it. A good PTA can help to transform a middling school into one that is thriving. If a PTA doesn't already exist, you could always set one up yourself. Here's what you need to do:

1. Find out how much support there is for a PTA. Speak to other parents, the headteacher and teachers. If there used to be a PTA at the school, find out why it closed.

2. Hold an inaugural meeting. Make your first AGM as interesting as possible to attract busy parents. Invite a well-known ex-pupil, or headteacher, or someone from a successful PTA to give a talk. Offer refreshments and childcare if you can. Publicize it as widely as possible.

3. You will need to form a small steering group – an acting secretary, treasurer and chair are the minimum requirements. This group should consider the PTA's constitution and make plans for an open meeting to launch the PTA.

4. Produce a constitution. This should describe the aims of the PTA, its membership, the size of the committee, election procedures and the need for an annual audit and general meeting.

There are a number of other things to consider when setting up a PTA. For instance, if it proves particularly successful at raising money for the school (in excess of £10,000 in a year), you will need to register it as a charity. Some of these arrangements may seem daunting, but every PTA in the country (and there are thousands of them) started this way.

You can get help with all these issues from the National Confederation of Parent Teacher Associations (their number is at the back of this book).

Parent governors

> I wanted to be a school governor because I work in quite a hermetic industry where we tend to mix only with people like ourselves, talking about our particular activity. The older you get in that industry the more you begin to feel just cut off from everyday life, and this is a way of reconnecting a bit with that. And because I live in a multicultural area I wanted to be a bit more involved in those kinds of issues.
>
> Jamie, father of Isobel, 11, Anna, 5, and Maisie, 4.

If you have been an active member of a PTA, you may fancy taking a step up and becoming a school governor. Being a school governor is a serious commitment and can be hard work, with meetings to attend, reports to read and difficult decisions to be made. The main legal responsibilities of the governing body are to:

- Take general responsibility for the conduct of the school
- Manage the school budget, including deciding how many staff will work there and how much they will be paid
- Oversee the curriculum, making sure it is balanced, and report on pupils' achievements and exam results
- Participate in the appointment of senior staff, including the headteacher, and regulate discipline of the staff
- Draw up an action plan after an Ofsted inspection.

The governing body usually meets once a term, and you may also sit on one or two of the committees that look in detail at things like finance, the curriculum or staffing, all of which adds up to a considerable time commitment. Some employers give paid leave for school governor duties, and employees do have a legal right to ask their employer for reasonable unpaid leave. Governing bodies are also allowed to refund costs for things like childcare or a carer for dependent relatives while you attend meetings. Altogether more daunting than the duties themselves may be the prospect of running for election with other parents at the school.

The governing body of a school is made up of:

- Parent governors
- Teachers appointed by other teachers at the school
- The headteacher
- Non-teaching staff elected by other non-teaching staff
- People appointed by the LEA
- People from the local community chosen by the governors.

You needn't stop at being a parent governor. Local authorities must now provide places, with speaking and voting rights, for Parent Governor Representatives (PGRs) on their main committees and sub-committees dealing with education matters. PGRs are elected by other parent governors to represent them in their area in local decision-making. Between two and five PGRs can be elected for each LEA and they serve for between two and four years.

Who to talk to when there is a problem

If you or your child has some problem with the school, the first person to talk to is your child's teacher, who may be able to deal with it. If it is a more serious issue, such as bullying, or if you are not happy with the way your child's teacher is dealing with it, then make an appointment to see the headteacher. Don't try and grab the teacher or headteacher in the playground when there are other distractions. If it is important then it needs to be discussed in a quiet environment.

This can be difficult, especially if you find the school environment intimidating, but remember that your child depends on you to represent their interests at school.

It might be useful to look at the home-school agreement, a kind of contract detailing the obligations of school and parents to each other. Home-school agreements outline what you can expect of the school and what the school staff can expect of parents and pupils in terms of attendance, discipline, homework, uniform and general appearance. They are not legally binding and parents do not have to sign them, but they may be a useful starting-point for discussions between you and the school. The school office will be able to provide you with a copy.

If there has been a serious incident at the school, it might be a good idea to wait a day or two. Don't rush in and say something in the heat of the moment that you later regret. Even when you are convinced of you or your child's case, make sure you go in ready to listen to what the teacher has to say. Children are not always reliable witnesses and, while they may feel they have been wronged by a teacher or fellow pupil, their sense of perspective is not yet developed.

In the case of an ongoing problem, a review of the situation may be a good idea. For example, if your child is finding it difficult to make friends, the teacher might decide to try and find her a playground partner. It is a good idea to agree to let a period of time pass and then to review the situation so that it doesn't get forgotten about once it has been discussed.

If you are concerned about a particular procedure or rule, then talk to other parents. Your child may not be the only one affected by it and you may want to take action together with other parents. If this is the case, it could be something to raise with the PTA or the governing body.

How a good school communicates with its parents

There are many ways in which a school can give information to parents. If you feel your school does not do enough then it might be worth tactfully suggesting some of these to the headteacher or the PTA. You could offer to help. The minimum you should expect from your school is:

- Regular information sheets to parents on outings and curriculum information
- A termly diary with important school dates in it
- A noticeboard for general, school-wide information
- Notes home from your class teacher about class activities, events and trips.

Now that desktop publishing and website design are affordable and easy to use, many schools have successfully introduced:

- A weekly newsletter
- A website/email bulletins.

CORPUS CHRISTI CATHOLIC SCHOOL

FRIDAY NEWSLETTER

Date 23rd October 2003

Volume 6, Issue No.7

DATES TO REMEMBER

No school tomorrow
Friday 24th October, 2003
Inset Day

Half Term
27th – 31st October

School resumes on Monday
3rd November at 8.50 am

(Children should be in the playground by 8.45 am)

Enjoy your half term break whether you are relaxing at home or taking a Ryan Air 01p flight for a few days!!

Merit Awards This Week

Class 1	Orla Mitchell
Class 2	Bridget Bradbury-Hickey
Class 3	Samuel Coyne
Class 4	Max Bergin
Class 5	Toby Redington
Class 6	Remi Delaye
Class 7	Guido Paloka
Class 8	Enrico Hallworth
Class 9	Camilo Montoya Moncado
Class 10	Yvette Botchey
Class 11	Sinead McCaffrey
Class 12	Medhina Mesfen

Attendance Figures for this Week

100	Class 3
99.6	Class 2
99.3	Class 7
99.2	Class 1
98.4	Class 5
97.8	Class 8
97.4	Class 4
97.5	Class 6
97.3	Class Nursery
96.0	Class 9
95.8	Class 10
93.1	Class 11
91.7	Class 12

Top Class This Week

Class 3

WELL DONE !

Week commencing 3rd November

Thurs 6th Nov   Class 11 Mass   2.15 pm

Fri 7th Nov   Class 1 Assembly   9.00 am

Corpus Christi Website

www.corpuschristi.lambeth.sch.uk

Look on the website for Class 3's Assembly held today.

E-MAIL

We are in the process of rebuilding our address book so if you would like to continue having the newsletter sent by e-mail, please send a request to:

office@corpuschristi.lambeth.sch.uk

THE SCHOOL CROSSING
WE NEED YOUR HELP

As part of the campaign to make the crossing safer for our children, a leading traffic consultant who is the friend of a parent has willingly agreed to give free advice to the school on what we should be asking. Transport for London to do. The downside is that we need to get together some information for him about how the crossings and the junctions of Brixton Hill/Trent Road and Brixton Water Lane are being used by.

A SURVEY!!
Would you be willing to give up a minimum of 15 minutes (ideally 30 minutes) of your time to stand on the roadside and count vehicles or pedestrians, no matter what the weather? It's not very hard to do, but you need you're wits about you and to be able to give you're undivided attention for the time you are counting. We need to count at a prearranged time between 7.45 and 10.00 am and 2 and 4.30 pm on Thursday 13th and Friday 14th November. We need almost 40 people to help. You will be fully briefed beforehand, at a meeting at 9.00 am on Wednesday 12th November in the music room, on what you need to do. At least four other parents from the school will be nearby when you are counting.

WE REALLY NEED YOUR HELP – please contact Judy Moullier (Lorcan Class 6 Pierre Nursery pm) or Helen Dias (Sophie Class 3)

Parents' Evening

Every child should have received a letter with an appointment for parents evening. If you have not, please let the office know.

St. Philip and St. James
PARENT AND TODDLER GROUP
'Little Rainbows'
Open on Inset Day Friday
24th October 10 –12 noon
Siblings and older children welcome.

Steve Gale's Urban Academy Football during half term
Monday 27th to Friday 31st October from 10 am to 3 pm every day
Cost £40 per child for the week.
This is suitable for Yr 2 – Yr7
If you have not returned your form turn up on the day at Loughborough School

Child care

A mother is seeking a parent/carer to collect 2 girls from school Monday to Friday and take them to the After School Club in Kings Avenue School. If you are able to assist please call Lorraine

Nanny part time is available on Monday, Tuesday, Wednesday and Friday. I have lots of experience and good reference, for more information please call Natasha

The National Childbirth Trust

Nearly new toy sale

**Saturday 25th October 2003
11.00 am to 1.00 pm**

St. Faiths Community Centre Bottom of Red Post Hill, SE24 Admission £1.00 children free

Parents' Association

Next Meeting
Monday 10th November
7.30 pm

Race Night

This turned out to be a very good night. The amount raised was £700

Cake Sale

Thank you for your support in sending in cakes for the cake sale. At the time of going to press the school is full of cakes and no doubt this will be another successful event!

A Big Thank you

Christmas Fair 2003

Will you have time to sort out your white Christmas lights this half term? If you are willing to lend them to us to decorate the hall for the Fair, please bring them in, clearly labelled, after half term.

Thank you

Next Craft Session

Thursday 6th November in the staff room 9.00 am. Donations needed of felt and zips (minimum length of 8") Please try to come and support us as it is not long to go now.

Christmas Fair 6th December

FIVE

What your Child Learns

The educational landscape has changed so much in the last 20 years that it is hard to remember what schools used to be like. Up until the 1980s the school curriculum was described in educational circles as 'the secret garden' – tended by teachers who were more or less left to their own devices and from which parents and even the government were effectively excluded. There were guidelines as to what should be taught in schools, but these were not statutory.

By the mid 1970s, the freedom of schools to run their own affairs was causing concern in the corridors of power, and in 1976 James Callaghan, the Prime Minister, gave a speech calling for 'a basic curriculum with universal standards'. When the Conservative government was elected in 1979, they started a process of school reforms, and in 1988 the Education Reform Act established the National Curriculum.

For the first time, schools in England and Wales were being told what to teach. Today, virtually every lesson taught in primary schools has to relate to the framework of knowledge and skills set out in the National Curriculum. The things that children are taught and their competence in them are measured by 'attainment targets' and 'level descriptions' for each subject. What goes on in schools is no longer 'secret' – all the National Curriculum documents are publicly available – but the jargon that surrounds it can make it seem inaccessible.

I think the National Curriculum seems to me to be on the whole working well, though I do feel that schools should have a bit more chance to play to their own skills. If they've got a teacher who is particularly interested in history, or children who are particularly interested in history there should be room to give them more history, or if they've got people with particular language skills they could perhaps start languages a bit earlier.

Jamie, father of Isobel, 11, Anna, 5, and Maisie, 4.

The national curriculum

The Foundation Stage

To make it more manageable, the National Curriculum is divided into blocks of two or three years called Key Stages. At primary school, children go through Key Stage 1 (Years 1 and 2, between the ages of five and seven) and Key Stage 2 (Years 3 to 6, from the ages of eight to eleven), which correspond to the infant and junior stages of primary education. Secondary school consists of Key Stages 3 and 4.

In September 2000, a Foundation Stage was added to the National Curriculum, demonstrating the increasing emphasis placed by the government on early years education. This stage spans the ages of 3 to 5, taking children from their nursery and pre-school education to the reception class of primary school. Although part of the National Curriculum, it doesn't divide into subject categories but consists of a set of targets called 'Early Learning Goals' which staff working with children should try and help them reach. The idea is that by the time they arrive in reception class, all children will have reached the same level of basic skills.

The Foundation stage is divided into 6 different areas:

1. Personal, social and emotional development. Helping children to be self-confident, teaching them how to ask for things, to know what is right and wrong, and also covering practical tasks like how to get dressed.

2. Communication, language and literacy. Encouraging children to talk confidently and clearly, to link the sounds they hear with the alphabet and to read and write some familiar words such as their name.

43

3. Mathematical development. Helping children to become comfortable with numbers, shapes, space and measurement.

4. Knowledge and understanding of the world. Learning about the world through exploring, observing and problem solving.

5. Physical development. Learning to move, play and dance in order to improve coordination and control.

6. Creative development. Exploring colours and shapes, dancing and making music, making things and telling stories.

In the first few weeks after your child starts reception class, the teacher may ask you to come in and discuss how he performs certain tasks, what he enjoys doing and what presents a challenge. The teacher will also be observing your child in the classroom, noting his strengths and weaknesses in the different activities. One of the reception teacher's jobs is to use all this information to draw up a 'Foundation Stage Profile' for each child, which is completed by the end of the year. This profile is used as a kind of marker – it used to be called 'baseline assessment' – against which the school can track a child's achievement over the years.

Key Stage 1

For a child of five years old, there is quite a jump from the play-based learning of the Foundation Stage to the test-driven rigours of Key Stage 1. The National Primary Strategy, which came into effect in 2003, recognizes this and has changed the way children are taught and tested in their early education. The Strategy is looking at ways of softening the transition – which it describes as 'too brutal' for some children – and giving teachers more flexibility in how they teach Key Stage 1. Generally, it encourages more fun and creativity in the classroom with the use of role-play and field trips for learning. This has been seen as a government effort to appear less controlling, urging teachers to 'take ownership of the curriculum'.

Even before the National Primary Strategy was introduced,

children at Key Stages 1 and 2 were taught quite fluidly. Unlike secondary school, where the timetable is divided into subject specific blocks of, say, a history class followed by a biology class and an English class with a different teacher for each, a primary teacher has the task of teaching everything – and as long as they cover the curriculum, it is up to them how they do it. For example, a project on the local neighbourhood may involve tasks and activities that cover parts of the curriculum in History, Geography, Art and Design and English. For every subject in the National Curriculum there is a 'programme of study' which sets out what the Department for Education and Skills thinks each child should learn. The trick is to plan activities and lessons that meet several 'learning outcomes' all at once.

Children within a key stage are working their way up levels which you could compare to the rungs of a ladder. In reception classes most children begin working at level W – short for Working Towards Level 1. During their two years in Key Stage 1 most children will climb up to Levels 1 and 2, and in Key Stage 2 they will attempt to scale Levels 3 and 4. This is the expected target of all primary children – the Key Stage 2 league tables show the percentage of children who have reached Level 4 in English, Maths and Science. In good schools brighter children will be extended beyond the expected level: the scale goes up to Level 8, and beyond that the category of Exceptional Performance is reserved for really high achievers.

These levels are defined in quite detailed ways. For example, for Mathematics the target level for 7 year-olds (Level 4) includes:

- being able to count, read and write numbers up to 100 and being able to count up or down from any starting number

- knowing the adding and subtracting facts for each number up to 10 – for example knowing that $8 + 2 = 10$, $10 - 8 = 2$, $10 + 8 = 18$, and so on

- knowing the pairs of numbers in tens that make 100 (so $20 + 80 = 100$, $40 + 60 = 100$, and so on)

- being able to double and halve numbers

- knowing their 2 times and 10 times tables by heart

45

- being able to say how many sides a named shape has and if it has any right angles
- being able to measure or weigh things using centimetres, metres, litres or kilograms
- telling the time to the half and quarter hour.

The government has national targets of what it wants to achieve in particular subjects. So, for example, in 2002 the target was that 80 per cent of 11-year-olds would reach Level 4 in English and that 75 per cent would reach Level 4 in Maths. The failure to meet these targets provided impetus for the National Primary Strategy, as it was argued that a plateau had been reached and that a new approach to primary education was needed. As part of the new strategy the government relaxed its pressure on Key Stage 2 and set back its 2004 target of 85 per cent of 11-year-olds reaching Level 4 to 2006.

Every year, children are tested at the ages of 7 and 11 to see how many of them have reached this level.

Key Stage tests

The new culture of prescribing and assessing what children learn in schools has had what many people see as an undesirable side effect – English children have become the most tested in the world. On average, if a child stays at school until he is 18, by the time he takes his A levels he will have sat around 105 exams in his school career.

The rationale behind the current level of testing is that it is an essential part of government strategy to raise educational standards. The government maintains that tests and targets are crucial in raising standards, and there is some evidence to support this view. An 11-year-old who leaves primary school having achieved Level 4 has about a 70 per cent chance of going on to get five good GCSEs – the standard benchmark of secondary school league tables – but only one in eight of those who do not reach Level 4 will get five good GCSEs.

In order to discover what level a child has reached, he must be tested. So at the end of each Key Stage children sit the tests commonly referred to as SATs – Standardized Assessment Tests – which measure how far children have come in reaching these targets. SATs usually take place in May, when children in Year 2 sit tests in English and Maths and Year 6 children are tested in English, Maths and Science.

The national league tables that are published each year in the papers and pored over by parents show the results of these tests and allow schools to be compared against the national and LEA average. The existence and use of tests in the league tables has been one of the most controversial elements of our education system, but despite the threat of boycotts from teaching unions and plenty of criticism, the government has stuck by them.

Arguments against national tests

- They are too stressful. Many parents and teachers say it is unfair to put exam pressure on children as young as 7.

- Nobody ever grew taller by being measured more often – even the Chief Inspector of Schools has criticized the focus on targets as 'excessive'.

- They squeeze out other subjects. Teachers end up 'teaching to the tests', leaving less time for other subjects like music or sport.

- They are a blunt instrument. Children absent on test days still count in the results, which do not take account of schools with high levels of inclusion.

- They are divisive. Children that do well show increased motivation, but those that do badly become demoralized and put less effort into their work.

Arguments in favour of national tests

- They improve standards. Since the introduction of testing, standards in literacy and numeracy in primary schools have risen considerably.

- They are comparative. The tests allow parents to track a school's performance and compare it with other schools both nationally and regionally.

47

■ Targets and tests have been important in improving many schools in deprived areas. The government argues that without these targets they would have continued to underachieve.

In theory, there should not be a 'pass' or 'fail' atmosphere around the SATs. You don't get a certificate for doing well – they are simply supposed to inform parents about their child's progress and tell the school about how well it is teaching the National Curriculum.

But the publication of league tables – usually concentrating on the best and worst achievers – has made them high-profile indicators of which schools are thought of as 'good' or 'bad'. And when schools spend so much time working towards them it is hard for pupils (and teachers) to ignore the fact that they are 'high stakes tests'.

Because SATs results determine a school's position in the league tables – and in many people's eyes its reputation – they can have a disproportionate effect on school life. In the Easter term, revising for SATs and trial tests can come to dominate the teaching. In the weeks running up to the SATs teachers give up learning time to do practice tests and extra revision. Some schools organize SATs Clubs where children can do extra cramming at the weekend or after school, and some parents enlist private tutors specifically aimed at getting their children through the tests.

A survey by the Institute of Education in 100 primary schools across the country found that teachers are concerned about the level of anxiety amongst their pupils at exam time. One in eight children showed signs of serious stress, including vomiting, bed-wetting and regressive behaviour. Childline say they receive about 800 calls a year from children, some as young as nine, worried about exams.

It's the children at Key Stage 2 that really feel the pressure. They're in an exam situation so all the tests have to be done in the hall which adds to the pressure. They'll also have been through the whole secondary school thing in September and October – interviews for secondary school and maybe taking tests for them as well. They will feel the pressure from their parents over secondary school. It's also their final year and they are maybe starting puberty, and on top of all of that they have these exams and then they are leaving. It's quite a lot for them.

We have a really successful breakfast club during SATs week to nurture them a bit. It makes them feel really grown-up. We do croissants, fresh orange juice, toast and nice jams. We just have breakfast and maybe ask them how they are feeling. A lot of the teaching staff go and the children can chat to their friends or the teachers.

Anna, teacher and mother of George, 7, Louis, 5, and Johnny, 1.

Although there have been cases of parents withdrawing their children from school during the week of the SATs, this is likely to be very unpopular with your school as it will have an adverse effect on their performance in the league tables. Good schools try to nurture children through the SATs – especially at Key Stage 2 – and the best thing you can do is help your child through the exams without putting too much pressure on.

Tips for stress-free SATS

- Try not to make a big deal of the tests.
- Don't compare your child's work or abilities with those of other children.
- Emphasize that every child's best is different.
- Don't let your child revise too close to bedtime.
- Make sure your child is getting enough sleep and relaxing out of school hours.
- Help him put in extra work in areas that worry him.
- Praise and encourage him in his work.

England is the only country in the UK to test both 7- and 11-year-olds. Scotland has never had key stage testing or league tables for primary schools, although it does have league tables for secondaries at the moment. Teachers there draw on a 'bank' of national tests for 5- to 14-year-olds and on a system of 'scientific sampling' that tracks the performance of a proportion of pupils. Even these tests are now to be abolished in favour of an emphasis on teaching rather than testing. Wales has replaced tests for 7-year-olds with teaching assessments, and is looking to make changes to Key Stage 2 testing. National league tables of schools do not exist in Northern Ireland or Wales for either primary or secondary schools, although in Wales individual authorities do produce tables.

Children not only sit tests at the end of each Key Stage but they also have a teacher's assessment. They can score differently in each. At the end of the school year if your child has done his SATs you will, as well as the normal school report, receive your child's End Of Key Stage Assessment results for the core subjects – English and Maths for Key Stage 1 and English, Maths and Science for Key Stage 2. These end of year assessments can be confusing, as they might include a different mark for a Test (spelling test) and a Task (writing composition), as well as the teacher's assessment. Ask the teacher if you would like anything explained to you.

Recently, it seems that the government has taken some of the criticisms levelled at over-testing on board. Part of the National Primary Strategy includes a trial whereby the way in which the Key Stage 1 tests are applied will change, and the teacher assessments will be given a greater role. Teachers will also be able to choose from a 'bank' of national tests (as in Scotland) rather than there just being one for all schools. If this is successful it will go nationwide.

What children learn

We often think of learning as a gradual, naturally evolving process – and the best teachers make it feel like it is. But since the introduction of the National Curriculum, teachers have had to tailor what they do to a framework of 'learning outcomes', which means every activity in the classroom will advance a child's progress along a carefully prescribed scale of abilities.

As a parent, ask your child what he has learned today. Try not to be tempted to ask what he has 'done' today because it's really important to talk about learning and schools are trying to do that. Children used to say 'we're doing the Romans this term' but we say now, 'We're learning about what the Romans ate and how the Roman times were different from our times.' Even from reception we try and

50

tell them, 'Today in this lesson we are learning to ... start sentences with a capital letter', or whatever it is. So they can think, 'Ah, so that's what we're doing.' I think for far too long we've thought, 'Oh, they don't need to know', but actually they do. I think education shouldn't be something that is done to them, it should be something that they are an active and integral part of.

Kate, deputy headteacher and mother of Eliza, 6.

Here are the subjects that children study at Key Stage 1 and the kinds of things they learn. At Key Stage 2 they learn the same subjects and cover the same kind of ground, but at a more advanced level.

English

English is divided into three areas: reading, writing, and speaking and listening. In reading they will learn about different forms of texts: stories, plays, poetry, non-fiction books and also dictionaries and encyclopaedias. In writing they will be expected to compose messages, poems, instructions, stories and notes.

Speaking and listening is basically about communication, how to listen to others, think about what they say, express

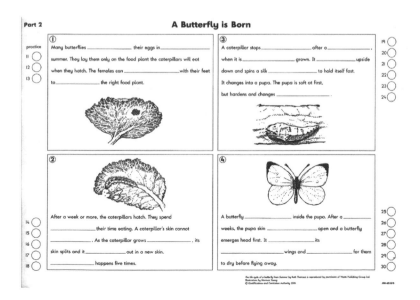

2.   *Scene from a Play*

Here is a short summary of a story:

> Sarah and Ben were supposed to take an old coin to the
> antique shop for their dad, to find out if it was valuable.
> When they were in the park, Sarah dropped the coin and
> they had to spend hours searching for it. Ben lost his
> temper with Sarah, but in the end they found the coin.

Part of the story has been turned into a **playscript**, which can be acted out.

Here is the scene in which Sarah and Ben realise they have lost the coin,
and start searching for it:

Scene 5

*At the gates of the park. Afternoon, about 2pm. Sarah and Ben are
saying goodbye to their friends.*

Ben: See you tomorrow, bye.

Sarah: (*touching her pockets and looking worried*)
It must be here somewhere.

Ben: What do you mean?

Sarah: (*nervously*) The coin...dad's coin.

Your task is to **finish this scene.**
(You do not need to write the first part out again.)

4

Planning Sheet

*This is for **very brief notes** to help you plan your ideas.*
Your notes will not be marked.

First, you might want to make a note of your ideas in this table.

How Sarah feels during the scene	
How Ben feels during the scene	

Now use your notes to help you plan your script.

Remember to think about:

- other characters in the scene, apart from Sarah and Ben;
- how to show what the characters are like through their words;
- how to give information about what the characters are doing while they are speaking;
- how to set out the playscript.

5

ideas and describe events and experiences. Children also learn to tell stories and take part in drama.

Maths

Children are taught about counting, solving simple problems such as addition and subtraction, and using diagrams and symbols as well as tables and charts. They also learn about shape, space and measurements, working with units of time, length, weight and capacity.

7 | How much money is in the money box?

p

8

53

Science
Children explore the life cycles of familiar animals and plants, materials such as wood and paper, and physical processes where they learn simple ideas in physics involving electricity, light and sounds. They learn about scientific enquiry – thinking about how things might work and then testing these theories or comparing results.

Design and Technology
Children look at familiar objects and learn how they are made and how they work. They also practise using the simple skills, tools and materials needed to make things.

Information and Communication Technology (ICT)
Children acquire basic skills such as using a mouse and keyboard, and become familiar with using computers to find, store and retrieve information.

History
Children learn how to place events in chronological order, look at significant dates and events, and about simple research skills. They learn how the past is different from the present and relate it to the different generations around them.

Geography
Through looking at their immediate neighbourhood, children learn to use geographical skills and resources, such as maps. They learn how and why geographical features change and how to care for the environment.

Art and Design
Children are taught to develop their own ideas and use a variety of different materials. They are encouraged to talk about their own work and that of other people, saying what they think and feel about it. They work with colour and pattern, line and shape, and texture and space. They look at the work of artists from different cultures and times.

Music
Children are taught to sing, to experiment with different sounds and to create their own compositions. They learn to

listen carefully, analysing the different sounds and tones of music from different countries and points in history.

Physical Education

This subject covers dance as well as games and gymnastics, teaching children how to follow rules, play safely and work in teams. In dance, children are taught how to move rhythmically and expressively.

Religious Education

All schools must teach religious education, but there is no national programme of study so it is not part of the National Curriculum and there are no targets for the subject at Key Stage 1. What your child will learn will depend on your local SACRE (Standing Advisory Committee on RE), who will have a 'locally agreed syllabus' to reflect the local population – a school with mainly Muslim pupils will take that into account in its RE lessons, for example. There are, however, national guidelines which say that RE should reflect the fact that the traditions in this country are mainly Christian, but that it should also include teaching about the other main religions in this country.

If you do not wish your child to take part in RE lessons or assemblies, then you have the right to remove them from all or just part of these lessons. If this is the case, then you should make an appointment to see the headteacher to discuss your reasons for this and how it can be done with minimal disruption.

Personal, Social and Health Education and Citizenship

We've been incredibly impressed by circle time and the emotional literacy of children today compared to our day. Some boys had been making flirtatious comments to some of the girls in my eldest daughter's class and the girls were finding it a bit oppressive, and as she related to me, 'We got together in circle time' – or bubble time I think it's called – 'and we discussed it with our teacher and we resolved the issue', and I was flabbergasted because that was a language we simply wouldn't have spoken.

Jamie, father of Isobel, 11, Anna, 5, and Maisie, 4.

There is obviously more to education than just knowing how to read and write and what is the capital of Cuba. The prevalence of drugs in society, the culturally diverse nature of Britain today and the fact that we have the highest rate of teenage pregnancy in Western Europe mean that our schools must be much more than academic institutions – they have to prepare children for life.

In response to the issues that face young people in today's world, the government introduced Personal, Social and Health Education (PSHE) in 2000, which aims to teach children the knowledge, skills and understanding to make good choices for themselves. In 2002, they broadened the scope of this approach by introducing Citizenship as a statutory part of the Curriculum in secondary schools. Citizenship teaches children what their rights and responsibilities are as members of the community.

PSHE is a non-statutory part of the National Curriculum and, where it is taught, covers all the Key Stages. It is concerned with four main areas:

1. All about Me. Self-esteem and confidence.

2. Citizenship. How a person relates to the rest of society.

3. Health. Nutrition, personal hygiene, exercise and how the body works.

4. Developing and Making Relationships. Caring for friends and family.

The school takes responsibility for the resources and strategies they use to teach PSHE and should consult with the parents and governors to decide what is appropriate for the age range and cultural identity of its pupils.

In primary schools, PSHE, is taught through the hidden curriculum and in specific PSHE lessons. The hidden curriculum is what makes up the ethos of the school – like 'This is how we care for people' or 'We are one big family and we look after each other'. It's how a school talks about things. Because a lot of PSHE is about relationships and respect and responsibility, it comes into the area of the hidden curriculum.

There are a lot of myths about PSHE, so at my school we had a parents' evening about it. We got speakers in, we showed them the videos that we use and gave them examples of activities that we do – to dispel the myth that it's all about bonking.

Anna, teacher and mother of George, 7, Louis, 5, and Johnny, 1.

Sex and relationship education

Sex and relationship education (SRE) comes within the remit of PSHE. Your school has to provide a written statement of its SRE policy, what and how it will be taught and from what age. The governing body is responsible for:

■ Consulting parents when drawing up the SRE policy

■ Protecting children from inappropriate materials, taking into account their age and cultural backgrounds.

There are national guidelines on what themes schools should cover in SRE. At Key Stage 1 these include:

■ Animals, including humans: how they move, feed, grow, use their senses and reproduce

■ The human body – recognizing and naming the main external parts

■ How humans produce offspring and how these grow into adults

■ Children should recognize similarities and differences between themselves and others.

At Key Stage 2 they should learn:

■ Life processes common to humans including nutrition, growth and reproduction

■ The main stages of the human life cycle.

If you have concerns about teaching in these areas, discuss it with other parents at the school and your child's teacher first. If this does not reassure you, then make an appointment to see the headteacher to discuss it. Parents do have the right to withdraw their children from SRE and PSHE, although very few do. Parents, however, are not allowed to withdraw their children from the elements of SRE that are being taught within the science curriculum, which includes learning that all animals, including humans, reproduce.

SIX

How your Child Learns

One of the great possibilities – and responsibilities – of being a parent is that you have the opportunity to make a positive impact on your child's learning. Successive studies have shown that a parent who takes an active interest in their child's learning is one of the most important factors in a child's educational achievement.

The effects can be startling. A recent study by the London School of Economics found that, no matter what their social class or income, parents could boost their child's results by up to 24 percentage points just by taking an active interest, such as by working with their children at home. The combined advantage of coming from a stable, middle-class social background and having parents who had stayed in education after 16 was only three percentage points. In other words, whatever your own level of education, your input can give your child a real advantage throughout her school career.

If you are going to be involved in your child's schooling, then it is important to know what and how they are learning. This chapter aims to shed a bit of light on the 'how' of learning without going too far into educational theory. It hopes to show you some of the challenges that face boys and girls as they progress through school and how you can help your child on her way.

All children learn at a different pace and in a different fashion. Some children learn better by rote and repetition, while others need only to hear something once to remember it. A hands-on demonstration can be the best way to help

Child A understand how something works, but a picture might explain it just as well to Child B.

Discovering your child's individual 'learning style' will go a long way towards helping unlock her full potential. Researchers have identified four widely recognized learning styles that occur in varying proportions in all of us. They are all useful ways of learning, but most people have a preference for one particular style over the rest. These are:

1. Kinaesthetic. The kinaesthetic learner needs to use her muscles to learn. She does not like to sit still and listen and finds it easier to remember things she has experienced. She will remember what happened or what was done rather than what was talked about. All of us start off learning this way.

2. Tactile. The tactile learner needs to use her fine motor skills when learning. So she may doodle or fiddle – and perhaps be told off for it at school. Tactile learners find learning to write easier than others.

3. Visual. The visual learner learns by seeing things and will enjoy looking things up in books and reading instructions. They remember things by writing them down and taking notes.

4. Auditory. The auditory learner learns by listening and likes things to be explained. She also enjoys talking, and may take a long time over descriptions and use a lot of repetition. Auditory learning is not usually fully developed until about the age of eight.

While all new teachers learn something about different learning styles, classrooms are traditionally dominated by the visual and auditory methods which cater to the needs of about 28 per cent of learners. Your child's teacher has up to 30 children in her class, so it may take her some time to become aware of each child's individual's learning style. If you are aware of these basic styles, you may get an inkling of your child's natural learning inclinations before she starts school and be able to pass on some useful comments to her class teacher. The more we know about the way our children learn, the more we can help them.

I think schools are increasingly becoming aware of different learning styles. It's the kind of thing that people have been doing in nursery and reception classes for years and years, and now that good practice is travelling up the school and becoming more common and also being more researched. People are going off and doing research into the way the brain works and how we learn. They are looking at children who might be finding it hard and asking, 'Why are they finding it difficult – is it because they need to see something visually in order to be able to do it?'

Kate, deputy headteacher and mother of Eliza, 6.

At the school where I teach we have done workshops for parents. We had a maths evening where we showed them examples of games we play. There isn't always time for that at school, and perhaps there should be. Parents can find out about it through magazines or at toy libraries – there are often professionals that can help them. But then often the people who access those services aren't the ones who need them most.

Anna, teacher and mother of George, 7, Louis, 5, and Johnny, 1.

Learning to read

One of the most dramatic things your child does at school is learn to read. Teaching a child to read and to enjoy reading is a lifelong gift. Children themselves seem to realize the momentousness of reading, as they are always very excited when they first start recognizing words.

The way your child learns to read is probably very different to the way you did – if you can remember that far back. Since the 1960s successive governments, have worried about the standards of literacy in this country in comparison with other countries.

ITA

In the mid-1960s, some schools began using the Initial Teaching Alphabet (ITA), devised by Sir James Pitman (grandson of the man who invented Pitman's shorthand), to try and help young children learn to read more quickly. This alphabet used the 26 letters of the standard alphabet as well as another 14 characters similar to those used in the dictionary guides to pronunciation to represent sounds like 'oo' and 'th'. Some children were taught to read with the expanded alphabet of the ITA until the age of 7, when they were expected to transfer their reading skills to the standard alphabet and accepted spellings.

The ITA was, in some senses, the forerunner of modern phonetic teaching methods, as it did try to give children a system in which words were made up of speech sounds, but it was never introduced systematically into schools. Many children found it very confusing to learn with one system and then be expected to switch to another, and it was yet more difficult for children with regional accents. It did, at least, acknowledge the fact that around one in seven English words are not spelt the way they sound.

By 1997, only 63 per cent of children were leaving primary school with the expected reading level. When such a basic skill is underdeveloped, it is to the obvious detriment of their learning in later years.

In an attempt to improve the standard of literacy teaching, the government introduced the National Literacy Strategy (NLS) in 1998, alongside the National Numeracy Strategy (NNS). The NLS introduced the systematic teaching of phonics in primary schools, and funded a training programme for Key Stage 1 teachers to improve their knowledge of phonics-based teaching.

Phonics is the association of individual letters and groups of letters with the sounds they make. So children at Key Stage 1 are taught to read and write in the following stages:

- to discriminate between the separate sounds in words (te-le-vi-sion)
- to learn the letters and the letter blends that are used to spell those sounds (bl-in-k)

- to read words by sounding out and blending their separate parts
- to write words by combining the spelling patterns of their sounds.

The NLS also introduced a daily Literacy Hour (to go with the Numeracy Hour of the NNS), which involves the class in teaching phonics and spelling, reading of texts with the teacher and independently, and writing independently. Teachers were initially sceptical about these impositions on their timetable, but the strategy is now widely accepted and in its report on the first four years of the strategy Ofsted said it had had a 'significant impact' on standards in English and on the quality of teaching.

Many schools now favour a structured reading scheme such as the Oxford Reading Tree. These carefully graded collections of stories have been created to introduce children to the most commonly used words gradually and with the use of much repetition. If you learnt to read with the rather humdrum Janet and John books, then you will find things have improved greatly, as the reading scheme books are humorous and imaginative.

Helping your child learn to read

To my mind, the most important thing you can do as a parent is read with your children. Read with them every night – and talk to them. Try not to sit them down in front of the television. People say, 'Oh, it's educational' – it's not. Children need to have conversations and be taught those social skills. But most importantly read. It's never too early to start reading with your child. Start reading with them when they are tiny babies and build up that regular thing. As a teacher, you can tell the children who read with their parents and the children who don't.

Kate, deputy headteacher and mother of Eliza, 6.

Some children learn to read with comparatively little effort, but for others (especially the youngest members of a class and those who are kinaesthetic or tactile learners) it can be a tougher task. In any class there will be huge differences between the most able (often the eldest) children and those who are finding their work more of a struggle.

It is also sometimes the case that children who have experienced a lot of reading at home and in nursery and have been encouraged to 'read' themselves feel a sense of failure when they first start to be taught to read at school. These children may have believed they were already reading, and when they suddenly realize they cannot it can be a blow to their confidence. They will need encouraging through this phase, as it can temporarily put them off the reading experience.

The most important thing to remember is that although your child may be struggling with his learning most children eventually 'get it'. Something usually clicks and the reading comes. If you are concerned about her lack of progress then talk to your child's teacher. Language-related learning difficulties like dyslexia are not always spotted early enough (research indicates that intervention by the age of seven can make a huge difference to later development), and difficulties with reading are too often attributed to laziness or lack of concentration.

There are many ways in which you can help your child learn to read. Even if your child is taking their time to start reading, avoid turning storytime into an intensive coaching session – too much pressure can be counterproductive.

Tips for helping your child to read

- Lead by example. Make sure your child sees you reading – both for enjoyment (such as a magazine or book) and for information (a recipe or street sign).

- Read to your child. This is one of the most important things you can do – it helps them to develop their powers of concentration and associate reading with pleasure.

- Try not to pass on any negative attitudes you may have to literacy.

- Make sure there are not too many distractions when you read. Turn the television and radio off, as background noise can limit concentration. Conversely, some children cannot concentrate in a silent environment, and soft background music may help.

- If your child is struggling to read, be sensitive to what

they want. Help them to 'sound out' the word and then supply it if they become frustrated. If they have had enough, then finish the story for them. Don't turn reading into a chore.

■ For some children, phonics will never make sense. These children will develop other strategies and these should be encouraged at home.

■ Praise them constantly in their efforts to read. Positive reinforcement works.

■ Use different opportunities to read, wherever you see words – in shops, in the car, walking down the street.

■ Don't feel guilty if you are too busy to read to your child every day. Something is always better than nothing.

A really useful way of helping your children with work is to think about what you are trying to teach them. Don't concentrate on them learning lots of different things. So if you are playing number snap, you wouldn't get them to write out the numbers, for example, and you wouldn't get them to concentrate on their handwriting and the way they are forming their letters. You just think, 'What do I want from this?' and you want one thing – you want them to recognize numbers. So you concentrate on that and you ignore everything else. When they are learning spelling, you don't worry about whether they are reversing their letters, you just concentrate on their spelling. That's your learning objective.

Anna, teacher and mother of George, 7, Louis, 5, and Johnny, 1.

Learning to write

At the same time as they start learning to read, most children are also beginning to learn to write. As they start to recognize letters you may see them making the outlines of letter shapes in the air with their finger, or attempting to write them when drawing or scribbling lines on a page, imitating adult joined-up writing.

The method by which children physically learn to write has changed over the years. Generally, schools try to build on the knowledge of writing that children bring with them when they first start at school. Any scribbles that the child does will be appreciated and the child will be asked to 'read' what they have 'written'. This takes into account the fact that when a child starts school they will already have had some experience of writing. They will have seen other people write and will have wanted to have a go themselves. They may even want to learn how to write their own name. All this should be encouraged but – as with reading – not enforced if the child is not interested.

It used to be that children learnt to print letters first and then joined them up into 'cursive' writing later on. Nowadays, more schools are teaching cursive writing almost from the beginning. Research has shown that cursive writing helps to develop the motor memory, creating an automatic response from the brain to the hand. Many people will, for example, have to write a word down before they can give the correct spelling, because their motor memory will tell them if it 'feels' right.

Tips for helping your child to write

- Encourage any efforts they make – praise a good letter shape even if the rest is unreadable!
- Focus on the content rather than the lack of punctuation or capital letters.
- Give your child plenty of opportunities to write. Once she is able to do so, ask her to write simple notes and messages in cards, and to add words she knows to shopping lists.
- Read a variety of texts to your child so she is exposed to lots of different styles of writing.
- Have a variety of different writing materials easily accessible to her.

Summer babies who are young for their year may find learning to write more difficult than the other children in their class, as their fine motor skills will not be so advanced and the physical act of holding a pen is harder. Help them practice their fine motor skills by playing with Lego, jigsaws and dough.

Learning to write involves not just the physical act of putting pen to paper but also the creative process of deciding what to write. Even at Key Stage 1 your child will be exposed to a variety of texts, so that she hears and reads different styles of writing including fiction, non-fiction and poetry. She will be encouraged to compose short stories and poems, as well as to use writing for factual information and self-expression through the use of diaries.

Learning about numbers

Of all the subjects their children learn at school, the one that parents are most concerned about helping them with is mathematics. There's good reason for this. It is estimated that half the adults in England are so bad at maths that they wouldn't even achieve the lowest grade at GCSE. The National Numeracy Strategy was introduced to address the problem illustrated by these figures.

At Key Stage 1, maths is divided into three broad topics:

1. Using and applying maths in practical situations.
2. Numbers – adding, subtracting, multiplying and dividing numbers, decimals, fractions and simple percentages.
3. Shape, space and measurement.

When children reach Key Stage 2 they start to learn about using and creating data in the form of lists, tables, graphs and diagrams.

All the areas above will be divided into smaller units and they may, as with all Key Stage 1 subjects, be taught through other subjects. Children are encouraged to do a lot of mental calculation, and when they write sums down they will be written horizontally ($14 - 8 = 6$) as 'number sentences' rather than vertically. This is thought to help them build up a mental picture of the sum.

During the numeracy hour the teacher spends 5–10 minutes on oral and mental calculation, followed by the main teaching activity lasting 30–40 minutes. The class will work in groups, in pairs or individually. At the end they will come together as a class to discuss what they have done, address any misunderstandings and summarize what they have learned from the exercise.

Tips for helping your child with maths

■ Take your time. Some maths concepts can be hard for children to grasp. If they don't get it, leave it, think of a new approach and come back to it.

■ Use the numbers that are all around us, on buses, houses, coins, clocks, football shirts, pop charts, and so on.

■ Remember to ask questions. Can you think of a higher number? What's that shape called? How much change would you get?

■ Be careful not to pass on any negative attitudes you may have about maths.

■ Play games involving dice and counting – Snakes and Ladders or Ludo are good.

Intervention programmes

An Intervention Programme is a course designed to accelerate learning in specific areas in Literacy and Numeracy. Children's progress in school is closely monitored these days, and special strategies have been designed to help children, who are falling behind to catch up. These strategies are called Intervention Programmes and have their own names like Springboard (a catch-up numeracy programme for Key Stage 2 children), Reading Recovery (literacy for six-year-olds who are struggling), and so on.

There are many different kinds of Intervention Programme, providing the flexibility to meet the needs of different children, either thorough one-on-one sessions or in small groups with a teacher or trained teaching assistant. Some of the programmes involve short blocks of ten 30-minute sessions while others, such as Reading Recovery, may involve daily sessions of half an hour for up to 20 weeks. Many children will just need one short Intervention Programme while others will benefit from ongoing help. The school should tell you if your child is on an Intervention Programme, and they should keep you informed of his progress throughout. Your child may be given special homework and other activities or games to enhance the work he is doing in school. Some schools will have sessions informing parents of how to help their child get the most out of the programme.

It's normal to feel concerned that your child might feel stigmatized by being singled out for special help. But the primary school day is so full of different activities in different settings – group and individual – that it is generally just seen as another part of school life, and most children enjoy the special attention they are getting.

Gender differences

For many years, there has been a gap between what boys are achieving in our schools relative to girls. Boys' under-achievement is not just a problem in the UK, as a recent Organization for Economic Cooperation and Development report found that the gender gap, at least in reading, was universal. At 15, girls had higher reading ages than boys in all of the 43 countries surveyed.

These gender differences are obvious from quite a young age. Girls usually talk and read earlier than boys and their fine motor skills develop more quickly. Once at school they are more motivated and progress more quickly. They are, generally speaking, more methodical in the way they work, so doing homework and revising for exams seems to come more easily. The neatness and order associated with girls' work is more in keeping with what teachers want, while the energy and vitality of boys are not always suited to the school environment.

Generalizations do come easily, but it is hard to ignore the facts of the test results. Even at Key Stage 1 girls perform better than boys. In 2003, boys were 11 percentage points behind girls in reading and 16 percentage points behind in writing at Key Stage 1. And the gap seems to widen as they get older: of the children who took their GCSEs in 2002, 57.8 per cent of girls got five A* to C passes, compared to just 47.5 per cent of boys.

Government policy is now specifically aimed at improving the situation. Since 1988, LEAs have been required to produce long-term strategies to tackle boys' underachievement, and Ofsted now includes an evaluation of this in its inspection criteria for LEAs. It has also commissioned a three-year research project to identify successful ways of dealing with boys' underachievement, as well as funding strategies like Playing for Success, whereby football clubs set up after-school study centres for primary and secondary pupils, to try to motivate boys in particular.

Some educationalists argue that it is not helpful to isolate boys' underachievement, and that we should look at under-achievement in general. Ethnic groups, such as African-Caribbean boys, are also underperforming in our schools. Figures for 2002 show that only 30 per cent of African-Caribbean pupils gained five or more good GCSE grades compared to 51 per cent of Anglo-Saxon pupils and 80 per cent of Chinese pupils, although girls of African-Caribbean background do much better than boys. In 2003, the government introduced a scheme called Aiming High to improve the underachievement of ethnic minority pupils. This includes extra funding and a pilot scheme targeting help at 30 secondary schools with a high number of ethnic minority pupils.

Supplementary schools

Saturday morning school is a thing of the past for most people – a throwback to the days when teachers wore gowns and pupils had slates instead of exercise books.

But in church halls, community centres and even front rooms across the country, thousands of children turn up to weekend classes at supplementary schools – a grass roots education movement that is helping to boost achievement and giving a crucial sense of identity to children from ethnic minority groups.

These Saturday morning schools exist on small chari-table grants and parental contributions, often employing qualified teachers. But the demand for them has increased, often in response to underachievement among pupils from particular ethnic groups and the low expectations some parents feel mainstream schools have of their children.

They are concentrated around immigrant populations in the major cities, but they are more widespread than you might think – from Japanese schools in Newcastle and Greek Cypriot schools in Somerset to Polish schools in Leicestershire and Nigerian schools in Liverpool. Altogether, there are more than 2000 supplementary schools in existence, ranging in size from just 10 pupils to more than 300. In London, some of the supplementary schools for children from African and Caribbean backgrounds have been in existence for thirty years or more.

Many supplementary schools offer cultural and language lessons alongside mainstream subjects such as Maths and English. The role of mother-tongue schools in reinforcing pupils' sense of identity is vitally important, as research has emphasized the negative effects on self-esteem among children whose first language is disregarded. The presence of positive role models in supplementary schools also goes some way to redressing the underrepresentation of Black, Asian and other ethnic minority teachers in state schools.

A survey by the government's Supplementary School Support Service showed that they are more popular than the Monday-to-Friday version. Of the 772 pupils they asked, only 12 per cent said they were bored at supplementary school – compared to 22 per cent at mainstream school. Three quarters were happy and found the work interesting. 84 per cent said it helped them with their work at mainstream school, and the same proportion said they got on well with their teacher.

Lower levels of attainment for all groups are due to a variety of socio-economic and cultural factors, as well as gender. 'Underfathered' boys may be harder to motivate at school, and a general street culture which does not see learning as 'cool' creates problems for schools. There may also be a problem of expectation and double standards when dealing with pupils from different sections of society. African-

Caribbean pupils, for example, are four times more likely to be expelled or excluded than other children. Studies have shown that high expectations are the common factor in schools where underachieving groups do well.

What to do if you feel your child is underachieving

- Show him education is important to you by spending time with her on homework and praising his efforts.

- Find a mentor – someone outside the family who they respect and who can support your child. Many areas and organizations have well-established mentor schemes.

- Help him organize his work so he feels more in control of it.

- Build on his strengths. Help him explore a particular subject he is interested in. Focus on the things he does best.

- Have high expectations for your child, but do not pressurize him. Don't bring your expectations down to his current level of achievement. Keep aiming for the level you think he is capable of.

- Use a system of rewards to help improve his motivation. Try to reward children with visits to places or activities they enjoy, rather than with material things.

Summer babies

Because of the way our education and admissions system works, some children start school just weeks after their fourth birthday. Many educationalists believe this is too young to start formal education and that at this age children should be in a play-based environment with more physical activity and freedom to choose what they do. Most countries in Europe start formal schooling at six and seven, usually after attending a kindergarten or nursery which provides some play-based educational content.

It can be very hard seeing your baby-faced four-year-old trot off to a full day at school. But it is worth knowing that, as a parent, you are within your rights keeping your child back from school until the term of their fifth birthday. However, this may prove difficult in practice and sour early relations with the school.

It is also possible, depending on the school's agreement, to negotiate 'flexi-schooling' whereby children attend school part-time. It is completely at the discretion of the school (that is, the headteacher and the governing body) whether they agree to this or not. To work well, you will need to have a good relationship with the school and you will also need to convince the LEA that you are making educational provision for your child on his 'home' days.

If you do have a summer baby, then it is a good idea to prepare her well for school as she will be in class with children almost a year older than her. It is likely that her fine motor skills will not be up to using pens and scissors as well as her classmates. You can improve general manual dexterity at home in a way that is fun. Anything that requires them to manipulate things practises children's fine motor skills. This includes things like dough or clay, jigsaws, Lego and building blocks, putting coins in a money box, using stickers or Fuzzy Felt and simple cooking and baking.

Most importantly, always remember the age gap. Children develop quickly at this age, so being ten or eleven months younger than the oldest member of the class can be a significant handicap. Don't try and hothouse a summer baby to make her keep up with the rest of the class. She will learn at her own pace and, proportionately, the age difference with her classmates will diminish as she gets older.

Homework

They start their homework at 6.20pm after *The Simpsons* has finished on terrestrial TV, and then there is a 40-minute break before *The Simpsons* starts on Sky TV at 7.00pm. So the three children are sitting out here at the kitchen table doing their homework in that break. The youngest one finishes first, as he has least to do and he goes next door and puts *The Simpsons* on. The other two scowl as he comes in telling them bits of the story and they have still got homework to do – it really annoys them. By 7.30pm I reprieve them as they've had an hour and a bit doing homework – they're allowed to stop what they are doing then and go and watch a bit of TV.

Sylvia, mother of Louis, 14, Justin, 11, Harry, 9, and Alex, 6.

It's no exaggeration to say that homework is one of the most hotly contested topics in education – both at home and in school. It has traditionally been a kind of barometer of educational standards: when there is concern about falling educational standards, the government will often encourage schools to pile on the homework. And when schools are doing well, a more relaxed approach is accepted.

Homework occupies a funny kind of middle ground between school and home – it's set in one place and done in the other. Some see it as a kind of educational overtime, adding to children's stress levels and making you the parent responsible for making sure it gets done. Done well, it can be a useful complement to school work and help children develop independent study skills that will benefit them in secondary school and their working life.

Independent schools have always been keen on homework, partly because it makes parents feel they are getting more value for money. But in the state sector, and especially in primary schools, it has not always been deemed essential. Research into the value of homework on a child's education is not clear cut. Some research suggests that it can be counter-productive when children get stressed over it and parents lack confidence about how to help or what it is achieving. In 1999, a study at Durham University found that there was no

Homework clubs

Fifteen years ago, homework clubs hardly existed. In 1991, when the Prince's Trust commissioned Professor John MacBeath to research what he called 'out of hours study support', he could find only three schools in the UK that had anything like it.

He deliberately shied away from describing them as homework clubs because of the negative connotations the h–word had for many children, so he called them 'study support centres' instead. The idea was that they should not only be places 'where kids went just to do their homework', they should be well-equipped and comfortable, conducive to rest as well as work. 'Turning kids onto learning was the basic notion', he says.

With funding from the Prince's Trust, the numbers grew. And after the 1997 election, the Labour government adopted it as policy, putting money towards a target of 8000 clubs nationwide. Another successful spin off has been the Playing for Success scheme of setting up study centres in football clubs and other sporting establishments.

The task, says John MacBeath, is to overcome old stereotypes of homework. 'When people frame homework they tend to do it in a traditional terms – you do work in school and you take it home,' he says. 'It's usually pretty boring, uncreative stuff they are doing. There's a big question mark over how valuable that is and how much it turns kids off. It's not homework per se but learning on your own and out of school that is important. That's where most learning takes place. The question is, how do you teach children to learn effectively without a teacher in front of them. In the big world of lifelong learning that's the single most important skill that people take away from school.'

evidence to suggest that homework boosts academic achievement.

The present government has been one of the strongest advocates of homework, which it sees as central to its drive to raise standards. It is especially keen on increasing the amount of homework done by primary school children, since a survey in 1995 which showed that 43 per cent of primary schools set no homework at all.

Arguments in favour of homework

- It allows parents to see what their children are studying at school and to help them with it.
- It teaches children in Key Stage 2 how to study independently and to develop research skills essential to later studies.
- It supports the work that your child is doing in school.

Arguments against homework

- It discriminates against less well-off or less well-educated families who may not have the time or resources that others do.
- It creates extra work for teachers.
- It tires children out and turns them off schoolwork.

The DfES guidelines for homework say that in primary schools children aged between 5 and 7 years should be doing about one hour of homework a week. This is most likely to be related to spelling, reading and number work. Between the ages of 7 and 9 years, an hour and a half is suggested as a suitable amount. The emphasis will still be on English and maths, but the range of subjects widens as they approach secondary school, and by the end of primary school children are expected to be doing half an hour of homework a day.

These amounts of homework are recommended, not mandatory, but your school should have a homework policy setting out rules and regulations. The homework policy of schools has been formalized not just because of government enthusiasm for it but also as a result of the introduction of home/school contracts outlining parental responsibilities towards the school and vice versa.

Sometimes with George I get up at seven o'clock and I lure him down with a hot chocolate and we do our homework then. It's good because it's a one-to-one situation. He quite likes coming down and he sits there and I'm milling about making a coffee. It's dramatic really – in a quarter of an hour he can write ten sentences, we have no scene and it's all fine. But if he does that at night we have five sentences, three scenes and loads of mistakes.

Anna, teacher and mother of George, 7, Louis, 5, and Johnny, 1.

Not all pieces of homework are written. For younger children especially, having to find and bring in an object relating to a school project or reading a book will count as homework. Any work done out of school that relates to work done in school is homework.

The DfES advises teachers that homework should be challenging (but not so difficult they will not be able to complete it on their own in the time allotted), linked to home life (using domestic tasks as examples or family members to help), and may be individualized (to suit everybody in a mixed ability class). Teachers should never use homework as a punishment (pupils will resent it), but non-completion should carry penalties (such as having in stay in during break time to finish the work).

With homework it is quality and not quantity that matters. Good homework is well planned, relates to a lesson and appropriate to the needs of individuals rather than of the 'finish it off at home' variety. At its best, homework should reflect the variety of learning styles that are used in the classroom. If homework is completed well it is important that this is acknowledged and praised by the teacher.

Helping your child with homework

One of the most direct ways you can become involved in your child's education is through helping them with their homework.

Whatever your own level of education, whether you have a degree or don't have an O level to your name, you play a really important role in your child's education. There are two ways of doing this. First, simply by being a parent. If your child knows you are interested in his education she will be more inclined to work better, is more motivated and appreciates the importance of education. Second, there are skills that you as an adult can bring to bear on her learning process.

When I arrived in this country I couldn't read. I've been to adult education so now I can read and I can write so I'm

77

trying my best to help them. Sometimes they correct me and say, 'Mummy, that's not how you write that'. Sometimes my son, who is in secondary school, asks me for help because he doesn't understand something but I have to say, 'Sorry but I cannot help you at all' because I cannot understand what children are learning at school at the moment. So we phone my stepdaughter who is 23.

Mila, mother of Andrew, 15, and Abigail, 6.

Tips for helping with homework

- Create the right environment – does your child work best with low background noise, in an informal setting, such as lying on the floor, or at a table and chair?

- Help her manage her work timetable – a regular time for homework is a good start.

- Encourage her efforts and praise the best aspects of her work.

- Don't do your child's work for her. The way your child completes her homework gives valuable information to her teacher about her progress.

- Talk about the work and ask your child how it relates to things she is learning at school.

- Discourage your child from copying if she is researching something. Discuss what she has learned and help her to put it into her own words.

- If your child is struggling with homework but has put in at least the required time, don't make her finish it if she has had enough.

- Give your child a lot of attention when she is doing her homework. Find the time to sit down and go over it with her.

- If you can't understand her homework talk to her teacher or enlist other family members to help.

- Be interested in her school day – talk to her about what she has been doing.

- Encourage any special interest she shows in a particular subject. Follow up with visits to museums or libraries, films or watching TV programmes with her.

- At primary school work should still be fun – don't force it.

SEVEN

A Child's Eye View

Schools can be stressful places. They are full of noise, rules and other people. For newcomers, school is an environment totally different to anything they will have experienced before. Before they get to primary school, most children will have been looked after by a relative, parent or childminder, or in a nursery or playgroup. They will be used to smaller groups of children and will, by the time they leave, have become used to being among the oldest there. At primary school they suddenly find themselves the smallest and youngest fishes in a much bigger pond.

School takes a lot of getting used to but in time most, if not all, children come to enjoy it. The children that have to be dragged into school are a minority – but all children go through times when they find school tough. It is here that they first make friends on their own, have to deal with non-parental authority, experience peer pressure and learn about success and failure, responsibility and stress.

This chapter aims to give an insight into the different challenges that the school environment presents to children and how to help them manage these challenges.

Talking to your child about school

When your child starts school it marks a watershed in his growing independence and developing a life outside the family. Respecting this independence means accepting the fact that you cannot control or know every detail of his school life. But it is also important to let your child know he can come to you with problems.

It will help your child cope with school life if he is used to talking with you about it. When something good happens, tell him how pleased you are that he told you about it, and if something bad happens or he is upset, don't brush it aside. Let him know he will be heard when he talks about school, even if it is negative. School is a very big and challenging environment for a child and being able to talk about it helps him deal with the issues he may confront.

Tips for talking to your child about school

- Ask specific questions like, 'Who did you sit next to at lunch?' or 'What did you learn?' rather than general enquiries such as 'How was your day?'
- Don't cross-examine your child about school. Talk around the subject – telling him about your school days may set them off.
- Take up any opportunities he raises to talk about school and discuss some of the issues around it like friendship, being good or bad at things and why we have rules.

Reflective Listening

When children find it hard to express feelings, it can be partly because they don't have the vocabulary to do it. Reflective Listening is a useful technique if you want to encourage your child to talk about his experiences. As the name suggests, it involves more listening than talking and aims to help the speaker find a solution to a problem or issue instead of presenting them with a ready-made answer.

In Reflective Listening the listener tries to understand the feelings contained in what the speaker is saying, rather than just the facts or ideas. So if your child says, 'I hate it that we have to do so much maths homework' the reflective listener concentrates on the emotion – the 'I hate' part – and restates or clarifies what has been said. As a parent we are tempted to find solutions or react by telling our children what to think. So we might say, 'Well you just have to do it' or 'I had to do much more homework when I was your age'. Using Reflective Listening your response would be something like, 'You really don't like your maths homework do you?' The conversation might continue with your child saying, 'Yeah, especially when we've been working hard all day at school. Why should we work when we get back?' Again the reflective listener doesn't try to answer the question but responds to the emotion by saying something like, 'You just want to relax when you get back from school'. Your child might then say, 'Why can't I do it before school?' – a solution, made at his suggestion, which you might then try.

In this example the listener has responded with acceptance of, and empathy for, the speaker and this has allowed the speaker to put his feelings into words and find his own solution.

Reflective Listening is better than questioning when talking to your child. Instead of accepting that your child does not like doing their maths homework, a question like 'Why not?' focuses attention on something that you as a listener feel should be discussed (i.e. their problem with maths) and demands a justification or logical explanation from your child. Children cannot always explain why they feel things and trying to do so can cause them to clam up.

Reflective Listening does not always work and if taken to extremes can become irritating, but it is a technique that allows your child to talk without being constantly told what to think, do and feel.

School refusal

Although we associate an unwillingness to go to school as something that only comes along with the heavier workload and exam stress of secondary school, it can also affect primary pupils. Some children love school from practically the first day, thriving on its challenges. Others may take years to really settle in – and a small percentage never do.

There is no clear definition of school refusal used by LEAs or schools, but common factors range from anxiety about going to school to a clear refusal to go. Symptoms can include panic attacks, vague illnesses, headaches and increased separation anxiety in general. Not enough research has been done to really establish how many children are school reluctant, or what causes it, but we know that a variety of factors cause anxiety at school. These include:

- The school environment – negotiating crowded corridors can stress some children out, as well as fear of specific places like the canteen or toilets.
- Conflicts with teachers.
- Unstructured time, like playtime, or lesson time spent working in small groups.
- Specific subjects – commonly PE, when children have to undress in front of their peers.
- Difficulties making friends.
- Bullying.
- Problems at home. Children often become reluctant to go to school if they are anxious about a parent at home because that parent is worried about something, depressed or subject to domestic violence.

Once a problem has been identified a good school will try to address the cause of it. Most headteachers recognize that there is a difference between 'bunking off' and suffering panic attacks, as some children do, at the thought of going to school. The more enlightened schools will have a designated member of staff concerned with school refusal/phobia.

The strategy used to help your child overcome his phobia will depend on where his particular anxiety lies. Changing schools is generally not a good idea, as you may find the problem repeated in the next school. Early action is the key, especially if your child is missing school as the longer your child is absent from school the harder it is to get him back. The following strategies have been useful in different schools:

- A 'buddy' system involving either another pupil or a teacher.

82

- Providing a 'safe' environment in the school where children can go when they are stressed out.
- Extra support in class.
- Creating an individual timetable to reintegrate children who have started missing school. Children may start going back just for a morning session, for example.

It may be that family support is called for. If a child is using a strategy of avoidance it is often because that is the way he has been taught to deal with things by the family, and so the family may need to work together to change behaviour patterns.

As a parent you are responsible for your child's school attendance, but the LEA is duty-bound to provide your child with an education so it, through the school, must take some responsibility for solving the problem. If you do not feel you are getting enough help from the school then you should take it up with your LEA.

Friendship

Before they start school most children have been guided in their friendships by their parents: usually they play with sons and daughters of their parents' friends, and other family members like siblings and cousins. If they have been at nursery then they may have made friends already, but will probably not have socialized with them much outside the nursery environment.

At school, children learn to make their own friends and to stand on their own two feet socially. They will start to lead their own social life, which is a positive experience for children as they learn the rewards of friendship – but it can also bring difficulties. Children at primary school often focus on a few friends or produce a hierarchy of friends, their 'best' friend, then their other friends and then the children they don't play with at all. For boys, girls may not even appear on the radar, and the same can be true for girls.

As a parent you cannot really control these things, but it is good to be aware of how your own experience of school friendships may be colouring your desires and expectations of your child's school relationships. It can be difficult for parents to put aside memories of being the last to be chosen for team games, and therefore they may attempt to compensate by making too much effort on behalf of their children. Those parents who had no problems gathering a lively circle of friends around them may find their child's comparative lack of playmates frustrating and hard to understand.

Tips for managing primary school friendships

- Emphasize to your child that there are lots of children in their class and school and they are all potential friends.
- Discuss what qualities make a good friend and what kind of things a friend does or does not do – this can help your child identify potential friends.
- Invite his friends over so you can see for yourself the dynamics of their friendship.
- If there is a friendship that you think is not good for your child, don't worry: it may not last – children's friendships can be quite fluid and things may change.
- If your child fights with his friends, discuss how you can get cross with people but make up afterwards and still be friends.

Difficulty with friendships

If your child does not seem to be making friends, try not to worry too much. There will always be children who seem constantly to be at the centre of things and top of everybody's party invitation list, but people make friendships differently. If your child has only one friend then he is already learning about friendships. Quality not quantity is important where friends are concerned.

Friendship stop

Children who are new to school or not naturally sociable can find it hard to cope with the free-for-all of playtime, and unstructured breaktimes can sometimes be a breeding ground for bullying or boredom.

Recognizing this, some schools have introduced schemes to encourage children to look out for their classmates and foster a sense of community. At Godwin primary school in Dagenham, east London, among the many bright murals and games in the playground, there's a cheerful wall painting of several people standing next to a bench. It looks like they are waiting for a bus – but this is not a bus stop, it's a Friendship Stop, a place where children go when they are on their own and want someone to play with.

Playground supervisors are easy to spot – they are the children wearing red caps with GPS (Godwin Playground Squad) written in big black letters on the front. If they, or any other child who is passing, see someone at the Friendship Stop, they will go along and talk to them or maybe teach them a game.

The children decided on their own rules for the playground – be gentle, be kind, play games that everyone can share and respect the grown-ups on duty. If there's a problem that the GPS can't fix, they call in the adults.

Through role play and counselling, the GPS volunteers, who are all from Years 5 and 6, get a crash course in conflict resolution for kids. They learn how to spot the signs of trouble through body language, and children are encouraged to sort out minor disagreements.

Godwin is not the only school to have such a scheme, but like all the others it has led to improvements in behaviour and fostered a more caring and responsible attitude among its pupils – something all schools would like to do.

If your child appears to be slow in making friends, then ask the teacher how he socializes in class. You may find that he plays well with children in school but by the end of the school day – especially soon after starting school when tiredness is a factor – he just wants to get home and immerse himself in the home environment. Alternatively, you may uncover some other problem. If he does not seem to be making friends you can try to help:

- Cultivate friendships by asking some of his schoolfriends over after school if you can.
- Encourage the friendships that he may already have outside school.
- Give him the opportunity to sign up for after school clubs – sometimes it just takes a change of environment for a friendship to be cultivated.
- Don't worry – making a big deal of it will only increase his stress.
- Remember: one friend is enough.

Lastly, remember that friendships always involve positive and negative experiences. As a parent you cannot protect your child from this, and neither should you try to. Developing skills to negotiate relationships, learning to cope with some distress and disappointment and developing a balanced perspective on friendships are all important skills that will serve your child well in later life.

Peer pressure and independence

Peer pressure is the desire that most of us have to be accepted by others of our age. As we get older we develop our own sense of self and right and wrong, but for children it can be hard to resist the pressure to fit in. Children of all ages dread ridicule or looking silly in front of their classmates or teachers.

Although peer pressure is often used in a negative sense, it can just as easily be used to achieve positive results too. A friend's advanced reading can be a motivating factor for a child to read more. In schools where bullying is a problem, peer pressure can be used to show that threatening and aggressive behaviour is not acceptable.

One way of teaching children how to resist negative peer pressure is to encourage them to be assertive. They need to know that everybody is different but everybody has the same rights: the right to be treated with respect, the right to be listened to and taken seriously and the right to say no. It is never too early to talk to children about subjects like this. Children have quite a heightened sense of natural justice so use it to teach them about rights – their own and those of other people.

You can also help children to be assertive by role-playing with them or discussing 'what if?'. At school they are bound to come across situations that are new to them, so it can be useful to have thought about these situations before they arise. So you could ask, 'What do you do if someone calls you horrible names in the playground?' or 'What do you do if someone falls down in the playground and hurts himself?' This gives children the opportunity to talk about things that may be happening in school and gives you the chance to teach them about the rights and wrongs of a situation.

Self-esteem

I like getting certificates at school when you stand up in front of the school and show them a piece of work you have done or something. When that happens you know you are achieving. One of the best things that happened at my school was when we won the cup. There are cups at my school and my class won the gold cup for attendance and punctuality. Children get prizes like cards or books and diaries. I got a diary and I got a £5 voucher last year because I came to school on time every day. The children that are on time every day get a certificate and a prize.

Kiana, 9.

An important part of helping children to resist negative peer pressure and enjoy their time at school is to build up their self-esteem. Self-esteem is the collection of beliefs and feelings that we have about ourselves and these start to build up from very early in life. Everytime a child reaches a milestone he feels a sense of achievement, which adds to his self-esteem.

As the child gets older he starts to form more opinions on his abilities and capabilities. As he becomes more adept at reading body language and understanding the meaning of words, these opinions will increasingly be influenced by other people's reactions – especially those of his parents. Be aware of how you speak to your child. Are you prone to criticizing or making sweeping generalizations like, 'Why do you always pick on your sister?'

I dislike competition in schools immensely. My son is on a low table because he has not learnt to read quickly and he knows that. He knows that because children come up to him in the playground and say, 'You're on level 3 and I'm on level 6'. That's what children are up against. I'm trying to protect him from feeling bad about being slow to read but at the same time I was slow to read as a child and it's not a problem because he is developing very much in the same way that I did. If children's self-esteem is taking a knock in primary school they are not going to learn.'
Julia, trainee teacher and mother of Daniel, 6, and Jasper, 4.

Although the classroom can cause self-esteem to flourish as children learn new skills, it can also give it a knock as they realize they are not the best at everything, that they sometimes get things wrong and even that not everybody wants to be their friend.

Nearly all schools introduce some element of competition into the lives of children. They very quickly work out the pecking order – who is better at reading, who is on the football team, who has lots of friends, who finds spelling tests easy and who has received the most stars or rewards from the system. This can be hard for children and it is up to you to put things in perspective for them. This does not mean that if your child says, 'I'm no good at spelling' you should respond with, 'Don't be silly, of course you are' if it's true that spelling is a problem area. You should give your child accurate feedback which gives them a sense of control and fosters a 'can do' attitude. A more helpful response might be, 'You're doing really well at school. Spelling is just something you need to practice to get better. We'll work on it together.'

Try these ways of building up your child's self-esteem:

- Give him lots of praise – encourage his efforts even if the results aren't so good.
- Don't get too competitive about it – try and involve him in cooperative activities where he sees people working as a team rather than in opposition.
- Be a positive role model – don't be harsh on yourself and try to guard against pessimism.

- Try not to compare your child to other children – and especially not to siblings.
- Listen to him – if your child frequently expresses negative or pessimistic attitudes, try to redirect his beliefs in an accurate and positive way.
- Create a nurturing home environment – a child who is experiencing lots of arguments, tension or violence in the home will suffer from low self-esteem.

Dealing with discipline and rules

I do too much spelling in school. If I was the headmistress I would make it so that we don't do that much spelling and that we have two lunch breaks and that you could bring in any kind of drink and I would change all the teachers apart from my teacher. They are just a bit bossy.

Imogen, 6.

Dealing with rules, discipline and authority is a relatively new experience for children when they start school. In contrast to most pre-school settings they have been in, schools introduce children to an explicit set of rules, sanctions and rewards. Most children become familiar with these rules quite easily and don't question them too much, especially in the early years.

In the latter half of primary school, children are more likely to question the rules that are handed down. Children of today are asked their opinions more than they used to be and are consulted more in their family setting, so the culture of most schools, which demands more or less unquestioning obedience, can be difficult.

I think that children respond to rules. I think rules make an environment safe. 'We do not spit', and 'We treat each other with respect' are good rules that I want my children to learn. I think rules are unhelpful when they don't serve a purpose for the child and when they are purely for the benefit of the adults. Then I think adults need to start questioning why they are putting their needs above those of the children.

Julia, trainee teacher and mother of Daniel, 6, and Jasper, 4.

Although most schools expect parents to back them up in matters of discipline, there will be times when you feel a school is over-reacting or being inconsistent in its approach. If you feel this is the case you should try and discuss it with a relevant member of staff. Don't necessarily let your child be part of all your thinking and conversations on the matter. If he sees a conflict between you and the school it can create an 'us and them' conflict, which won't support his learning.

How the school deals with discipline will depend primarily on the headteacher. If discipline is becoming a real problem a good school should work with the parent and the child to negotiate targets for behaviour, with rewards for behaving well. The child should be part of this process and, in some extreme cases, there may need to be flexibility in the curriculum.

All schools have a discipline policy which should have been drawn up with the involvement of the whole school community. It usually contains a fairly general wish list about respect for others, what kind of community the school wants to create and how members of the community should be treated. There may also be more specific examples of what kinds of sanctions various types of behaviour might invoke, detailing what will merit permanent exclusion and what type of system there is for written warnings. It will probably also include the uniform policy.

School councils

The idea that children can have a say in the way schools are run is a relatively new one. But it is gaining ground, and hundreds of schools now give their pupils the chance to debate matters that affect them and to recommend changes to school policy and practice. School councils usually consist of one representative from each class, elected by their classmates, who meet on a termly basis, although the exact arrangements vary from school to school.

A successful school council is much more than a talking shop. By canvassing opinion, campaigning, attending meetings and making decisions, it helps the children involved develop useful life skills as well as giving all the school's children the feeling that they are involved in the running of their school and that the school values their opinion.

Schools Councils UK is the national organization devoted to helping to set up and run school councils. It grew out of a project on a housing estate in Liverpool in the early 1990s where many children complained that their school did not listen to their opinions. It now employs six full-time staff to advise and support school councils, and provide training and resources.

They advise schools thinking of setting up a school council to:

- Give it time – many schools took years before they found a system that worked for them.
- Provide training – for pupils and teachers who act as coordinators.
- Build from the bottom – short, weekly class meetings are a good way to get children enthusiastic.
- Start small – don't begin with a big project.

Bullying

Raising children's self-esteem and teaching them how to be assertive can help prevent them becoming the victim of bullies and from becoming bullies themselves. If your child has been taught about rights then he is more likely to talk to someone if he is being bullied. Children need to know that if they are being bullied they should not stay silent but ought to talk to their parents, or a teacher. Research shows they are more likely to confide in a parent than a teacher, so take any reports of bullying seriously.

They didn't accept me because of my glasses and I couldn't play football and I didn't really like sports. I came in Year 3 so it was very hard to make friends as they had already made friends and soon there were rumours spread about me and things like that so it was very hard.

Most of it was just verbal. One of the worst bullies was actually the son of a teacher. I thought things would just get worse if I told so I didn't tell anybody. I did tell the teachers in the end but the rumours had spread so far that there was virtually nobody in the school who would be my friend. There were only about three people who actually did stick up for me and they were really good friends.

Justin, 11.

Bullying can take different forms – physical intimidation, name-calling, isolation from the peer group, spreading rumours, text-messaging or racist bullying. As a parent, you should be vigilant and be aware of what could be signs of bullying:

- Unexplained cuts and bruises
- An unwillingness to go to school
- A desire to be driven to school or to go by a different route
- In younger children, a wish not to be left alone in the school playground
- A falling off in schoolwork and lack of interest in school generally
- Mood changes and withdrawal
- Behavioural changes – reappearance of a stammer, loss of appetite, bed-wetting, etc.
- Things going missing without any convincing explanation – bits of uniform, dinner-money or stationery
- Your child asking you for money
- Dramatic changes in friendships at school.

With any of these things there could be a perfectly innocent explanation that is nothing to do with bullying. But if your child says he is being bullied then you must take it seriously, as you could be his only chance of changing a miserable situation.

When he was being bullied he was very moody. He'd come home in a temper and take it out on the younger children. I think that was the effect of coping with the bullying at school. It's difficult to tell sometimes whether it's actually the bullying that's doing it or whether it's just sibling rivalry, but more often than not I'd find it's because of something being said at school.

Sylvia, mother of Louis, 14, Justin, 11, Harry, 9, and Alex, 6.

If you suspect that your child is being bullied but he hasn't said anything, then try to find out more about how he spent his day. Who did he play with at playtime? What games did they play? Did he enjoy it? Would he like to play with someone else? Is he looking forward to school tomorrow? You could even try subtly finding out from his friends if there is a problem.

> I was bullied in school and because of that I learned nothing. So it's difficult for me. I don't know how I'd deal with it if my daughter was bullied. My son was bullied for two years and I struggled. I didn't know what to do. My son said to me he didn't want to go to school and he said he'd prefer to die than stay at school. They called him Bugs Bunny because of his teeth. He had an accident when he was 18 months old and it is too early to do an operation for them. But they give him a hard time because of it.
>
> Mila, mother of Andrew, 15, and Abigail, 6.

If you discover that your child is being bullied it is important you don't try to approach the bully or his parents. Don't go marching into the school all guns blazing, however much you may want to rush to your child's defence. This is probably exactly the reaction your child was dreading. Try a more measured approach instead:

- Talk to your child and try to agree with him any action that should be taken.
- Discuss how he might handle the bullying by avoiding eye contact, ignoring or avoiding the perpetrator, and so on.
- Suggest that he keeps a diary of any bullying incidents. Regaining some control over the situation will be an important part of solving the problem for your child.
- Look at the websites aimed specifically at children that talk about bullying, why it happens and how to deal with it (listed at the back of this book). This will help children know that they are not alone and feel empowered to try and deal with the bullies.

■ Explain that it is not his fault that he is being bullied. Tell him that people can be bullied for a particular reason or for no reason at all, but that it is never right and is always the fault of the bully.

Next, approach the class teacher with your concerns. You can ask your child if he wants to be at the meeting, but if he doesn't then that is okay. Don't be confrontational as teachers are not omnipresent and if you have only just discovered there is a problem there may be no reason for them to have noticed it.

Ask the teacher to keep an eye out and to ask the playground supervisors to watch out for your child in the playground. Most bullying in primary schools takes place here, while in secondary schools there is more opportunity for bullying to take place outside the school. Encourage any friendships your child has so that he is not isolated in the playground.

If the bullying continues then write a note to the teacher and ask for it to be put on your child's file. How schools react to accusations of bullying will vary greatly. Since 1988 headteachers have been under a legal duty to draw up an anti-bullying policy. Ideally, this should have involved the whole school community – parents, governors, staff and children. This does not extend to Scotland, although headteachers there are encouraged to do so. You should also ask for a copy of this anti-bullying policy.

If the problem is ongoing then make an appointment to see the headteacher. If your child has kept a diary of incidents, take it with you. Ask the headteacher what action he suggests can be taken and how it will be monitored. Once you have seen the headteacher, make sure that a date is fixed to review the situation. The school needs to know how seriously you take it. Your child has the right to be educated without being intimidated or harrassed, and these rights are enshrined in various laws.

The bullying may not stop immediately, and you may have to be persistent. If the problem continues then you should write to the Board of Governors, and if you really feel the school is ignoring the problem then contact the LEA. If your child is being bullied then the chances are that other children are too, and it is in everyone's interest that the problem is sorted out.

Research in the early 1990s revealed that one in ten primary school children is bullied up to several times a week, with one in four being bullied more than once a term. If the bullying is happening at a certain time of day or location, then ask that there is extra supervision at those danger points. If your child can be separated from the bully then that can help to break the cycle. A 'buddy' system, whereby older children look out for younger ones, can help. Some schools use innovative measures such as 'bully courts' made up of peer students that decide what should happen to fellow students accused of bullying. This may be bit radical for your school, but generally the following seem to help:

- Use peer pressure in a positive way, with peer support systems so that older children learn to look out for younger ones, and take pride in it.

- An extension of this is to be a 'telling' school, which means that even if the victim is too afraid to tell the teachers the bystanders know it is their duty to do so and they will not be accused of 'telling tales'.

- Talk about bullying in assemblies and within the curriculum, such as in PSHE citizenship, RE or drama.

- Use leaflets and posters to re-inforce the anti-bullying ethos.

- Take reports of bullying seriously. Children need to know that they will be listened to if they do report bullying.

And lastly, if your child is very distressed then make an appointment to see your GP, who may decide to refer you on to professional help. Although it is a minority of cases, some children have been driven to suicide as a result of playground bullying.

If your child is a bully

Almost worse than having your child bullied is knowing that your child is doing the bullying. Children that bully can come from any background, social class or cultural group. They may be doing so because of a lack of self-esteem, to fit in with a group, because they don't know how else to relate to their peers or because they themselves are being bullied.

They may be experiencing problems and so act out their feelings of aggression on other children.

Whatever the case, they have to be told it is wrong and find other ways of communicating their fears, aggression or anger. If your child is bullying it is important to get him to empathize with his victims, but also to address the reasons why he feels the need to bully. He needs to know that his bullying is making his victim unhappy and is probably making him unhappy too.

If your child is bullying other children, it is important you work with the school to try and address the problem together. Think about any changes there may have been in your child's life that may have caused upset: is he witnessing lots of aggressive behaviour that could be encouraging him? Is he himself being bullied? A Childline survey found that 15 per cent of primary school students had not only been bullied in the last year but that they themselves had bullied in that time as well.

If talking to your child and involving the school does not bring results then it would be worth contacting the organizations listed at the back of this book. Some of them run courses for both children who have been bullied and for children who bully.

Stress at school

While your schooldays can truly be the best days of your life, it is obvious that school can be a challenging environment for children. They can, with your help, cope with most of these things very well, but research shows that children in our schools are increasingly stressed.

A lot of the stress can be blamed on exams, so expect them to be more uptight in the years they take their SATS. A survey in 2002 undertaken for the Liberal Democrats found that 55 per cent of 7-year-olds preparing for their Key Stage 1 SATs showed signs of stress.

You can help your child to deal with stress in the following ways:

- Be aware of what stresses him out about school and help him to develop coping mechanisms. So if he panics about getting his homework in, make sure that the conditions are right for him to finish it in good time and well.

- Talk to him about school so he is able to offload any worries he has.
- Make sure he is getting enough sleep.
- Don't encourage competition. Value his work for its own sake and for the effort he puts in.
- Cultivate interests and friends outside school so that the school environment does not totally dominate his life.
- Try to be relaxed yourself about the challenges he faces. If your reactions are over the top he will pick up on this or stop trying to involve you.

This last point is the most important of them all. It is easy to blame schools and the system for increasingly stressed children, but parental expectations also play an important part. Parents are much more involved in their child's schooling than before, and as a parent the demands and expectations you make of the system can very easily appear to be demands and expectations of your child.

My son's teacher says, 'Oh you're a hard mother to please. Your son is achieving well and you're not pleased with it.' I want him to do more not for me but for himself. You know it's there for him to take. When I was a child it was not there for me to take, I had to work really hard to do it. Because in my country when it was my time to go to school I only go two or three times a week because my parents said I have to earn money to buy food. I stopped going to school at twelve years old because I had to go to work to feed my whole family. But for them it's there for the taking. I say to him, 'Don't wait for it to come down to your lap, go for it, take it for yourself.' That's what I keep telling them.

Mila, mother of Andrew, 15, and Abigail, 6.

And finally . . .

Primary schools have a great pastoral responsibility towards the children in their care, and this is recognized in the National Curriculum. All the issues discussed in this chapter are covered in the Personal, Social and Health Education (PSHE) part of the Curriculum. This includes Citizenship and Sex and Relationship Education, and is concerned predominantly with relationships.

It aims not only to help children understand their bodies and how to look after them, but also to develop an awareness of behaviour in themselves and others. It helps them develop opinions and the skills to put this across. It looks at concepts like responsibility, respect and cooperation and sees how they apply this to their own lives and the relationships around them.

EIGHT

The Teacher's Perspective

As a profession, teachers have generally – and undeservedly – suffered from a poor image. Saintly, self-sacrificing figures like Miss Jean Brodie and Mr Chips are seen as a thing of the past, and public perceptions have shifted towards the scruffy incompetents that inhabit the fictional schools of so many television dramas.

As parents, our personal opinion of teachers most likely depends on those we encountered at school, making it highly subjective as well as out of date. Teachers in the UK do not enjoy the status accorded their colleagues in other countries, but anyone who has spent any time in schools will tell you that the vast majority of teachers are devoted to their job and go about it with great care and skill.

This chapter is intended to give you some insight into a teacher's job, and how you as a parent can work with teachers to support your child's education.

Training

Every day is different. You are very independent, you can create your own structure. You have such flexibility, you're having to think on your feet and be really responsive to the children. There's a lot of performance in it too. I've got a degree in English and Drama so I love that whole acting and performance side of it. All teachers are different but I can only do it in the way that's natural to me and it's great. It's a great job.

Kate, deputy headteacher and mother of Eliza, 6.

To become a teacher you need to gain Qualified Teacher Status (QTS), and to do this you need to complete an Initial Teacher Training (ITT) course. There are three main ways of achieving this.

- The undergraduate route. A teaching degree (BEd) lasting three or four years – common for primary teachers.

- The postgraduate route. A one year Postgraduate Certificate of Education (PGCE) course taken after completing a degree. Secondary school teachers, who need a degree in the subject they teach, often qualify this way.

- The employment-based route. Postgraduates who spend a year working as an unqualified teacher while they train or classroom assistants who then do a course to become teachers. This is called SCITT – School Centred Initial Teacher Training.

All newly qualified teachers (NQTs) will have spent some time doing teaching practice. If you do a teaching degree, then you have to spend about 24 weeks of a three-year course in a school – people on a primary PGCE course will have spent about 18 weeks. During their first year in school, called the induction year, NQTs are mentored by a more experienced teacher to show them the ropes and to ensure their work is up to standard and that the children in their class are being properly taught.

I was motivated by my son's nursery which is an extremely good example of best practice – it's very inspiring. I actually didn't know that teaching could be like that until I started looking round for schools, nurseries and the rest of it. It exemplifies the early years ideals of learning through play. I thought, 'I really like being here and my kids like being here – I would like to do this.' Which is why I've applied for early years training.

Julia, trainee teacher and mother of Daniel, 6, and Jasper, 3.

The quality of teacher training has improved out of all recognition in the last 20 years, and teachers are expected to continue training and developing their skills throughout their careers. To gain QTS teachers are expected to:

- Show the values, attitude and commitment expected of teachers.
- Know and understand the Curriculum for the age range for which they are trained, and show confidence in teaching it.
- Understand how children learn and how pupils should progress and what is expected of them.
- Show skills in behaviour management, classroom control, lesson planning and pupil assessment and monitoring.

Vetting

Before they can start work, anyone whose job brings them into contact with children or vulnerable adults has to be cleared by the Criminal Records Bureau. Teachers and all school support staff have to be vetted in this way, in order to ensure that adults who are a danger to children are not allowed to work in schools. The names of those who are deemed to pose a risk to children – because they have been convicted of or suspected of child abuse – are kept on a register called List 99. It used to be the case that schools wanting to take on a new member of staff checked with the Department for Education to make sure that person was not on the list, and then checked with the local police force. But after the abduction and murder of Jessica Chapman and Holly Wells in Soham in 2003, the rules were tightened up and the government decided that all existing staff needed to be cleared by the CRB, a centralized national checking service set up in April 2002. Delays in the system meant that thousands of staff were unable to start work in September 2003 until their checks – called disclosure – had been processed by the CRB. A standard disclosure checks all past criminal convictions (including spent convictions), cautions and warnings as well as whether or not the person is on the DfES list of people unsuitable for work with children.

Primary school teachers are trained to teach the core Curriculum – English, Maths and Science – as well as at least one other specialist subject. Although primary teachers teach across the Curriculum, every school has subject coordinators who oversee the school's teaching of each part of it.

Teacher shortages

There's no doubt that – personally if not financially – teaching can be one of the most rewarding jobs in the world. But it's not an easy job, and in recent years it has suffered from a recruitment problem in general and, at secondary level, from shortages in particular subjects.

Of the 42,000 primary teachers that left the profession in 2002, 59 per cent blamed workload as the main factor. Another survey from the same year found that of every hundred people to enrol on a teacher training course, 40 drop out without completing it, 10 leave teaching within three years of starting work and 15 move into another branch of education. Only one third will pursue a long term career in teaching. But those that do usually find it one of the few professions to offer the potential to genuinely change people's lives.

In recent years, schools in Britain have suffered from teacher shortages, forcing some LEAs to start recruiting directly from Australia, New Zealand and the US. Certain schools (especially secondary schools in London and the South East where the cost of living is high) and certain subjects (particularly Maths, Languages, Sciences and IT, where qualified people can earn much more in other jobs) have been hardest hit.

The situation is not as serious as it was a few years ago, thanks in part to a system of 'golden hellos' – financial payments of £4000 for teachers of shortage subjects and other areas. For example, male primary teachers also qualify for this payment because they are underrepresented – at the moment only about one in seven primary school teachers is male. The lack of male role models in primary schools has been identified as a possible reason for boys' underachievement.

Higher up the career ladder, new grades such as the Advanced Skills Teacher have been introduced to keep the best teachers in the classroom and pay them more if they can demonstrate their ability.

The various incentives have, to a certain extent, worked. In 2002, 31,000 people registered for teacher training courses with the TTA, the highest figure for 12 years. More people are switching from highly paid professional jobs to do something they feel is more worthwhile and rewarding.

> I think teaching is a much bigger job now than it used to be. My mum was a teacher and she taught at our primary school and we used to go home with her and if she did any work at home it was something like cutting out a decoration for the classroom. It's just not like that now. I met someone last week and she said 'Oh you're a teacher, that's nice. Do you drop the children off on your way to school and pick them up on your way back?' Well, I get to school for eight and I get home at half past six.
>
> Anna, teacher and mother of George, 6, Louis, 5, and Johnny, 1.

These days there is a lot more to teaching than simply what goes on in the classroom. Since the introduction of the National Curriculum and the many government initiatives that have followed it, the increasing level of bureaucracy in schools has left teachers with a mountain of paperwork.

Children's progress in relation to the different levels of the Key Stages is recorded in great detail every step of the way. These written pupil assessments are only half the story: there are also the lesson plans, the marking, schemes of work, numeracy plans, literacy plans, preparing children for SATs, liaising with other professionals in social services, health services and special needs, and much, much more.

> The National Literacy Strategy, the National Numeracy Strategy, the National Curriculum, the Foundation Stage curriculum – for me I welcome all of that change. It's about always trying to find new ways. The new stuff is all about the different learning styles – being a visual learner, a kinaesthetic learner, or an oral learner – and about trying to develop a multi-sensory approach to teaching. It's about

getting away from chalk and talk, which suits some children very well but which other children find really difficult to access.

Kate, deputy headteacher and mother of Eliza, 6

According to a General Teaching Council survey of 70,000 teachers in 2002, around a third of teachers expect probably or definitely to have left the profession in the next five years. The top three factors that demotivate them are the workload, the number of new initiatives and the testing and targets culture – each mentioned by more than a third of teachers. The majority of teachers had lower morale than when they entered the profession.

Relations with parents

Part of your job is obviously dealing with parents, and parents can get anxious and stroppy and can become aggressive. Sometimes you are having to say quite difficult things to parents about their children and that can be very hard. If you're not completely committed to the job and completely passionate about the job you really shouldn't be doing it, because you are short-changing the children.

Kate, deputy headteacher and mother of Eliza, 6.

Of the 70,000 teachers surveyed by the GTC in 2002, 54 per cent said they chose it as a career because of the chance to work with children and young people. But teachers also have a crucial relationship with the parents and carers of their pupils.

Sometimes this can be an uneasy relationship. The conduct of some parents and their lack of support was cited as a demotivating factor by 11 per cent of teachers. Nine out of ten teachers said they found it harder to control parents than their children, and felt that 21 per cent of parents had not much or no respect at all for them – compared to 14 per cent of pupils and five per cent of colleagues. Very occasionally, the relationship between teachers and parents breaks down completely – and a growing number of parents who have threatened or used violence against teachers are being banned from school premises.

Violence against teachers has become a serious problem for the profession, with several hundred assaults on teachers every year. Although the majority of attacks are by secondary age boys, parents commit around five per cent of attacks. Teaching unions have announced a zero tolerance approach to assaults from parents.

It can be difficult for parents to accept that their children are not doing as well academically as they hoped, or that their behaviour is not what it should be. Some parents react by blaming the teacher. Occasionally, they may have a point. But parents who get aggressive are not doing anything to help their child's education or resolve the problem. Serious concerns should be taken to the headteacher. In 2000, the government said that parents who abuse, threaten or assault teachers also risk having their child expelled as well as possible legal action which could result in a banning order, a fine or, in serious cases, a prison sentence.

Classroom assistants

Most primary classes will have at least one full-time classroom assistant, also known as a learning support assistant or teaching assistant. It is their job to support the teacher, and they work under his direction. Usually they will be attached to one class, although sometimes their work is organized so they work around the school with different groups. Their duties usually include the following:

- Giving extra time and help to children with special educational needs or children on intervention programmes
- Working with groups of children when the class is divided up
- Helping the teacher set up and prepare activities with the children
- Some classroom assistants help the teacher plan lessons and assess the children.

At the moment, classroom assistants do not take whole classes on their own unless perhaps the teacher is unwell or has to be absent at short notice. The government has plans to change the role of classroom assistants which would allow them to teach a whole class on their own, but this is being resisted by teaching unions.

Classroom assistants do not have to be trained, although many will have childcare or education qualifications (six per cent of them have degrees) and the system for classroom assistants is being increasingly formalized with a range of qualifications aimed at classroom assistants.

Other staff

As well as classroom or teaching assistants there is a whole range of other support staff and roles that teachers take within a school. The mains ones are:

- SENCO – The Special Educational Needs Coordinator. Responsible for the support and teaching of children with SEN. In larger schools this is a full-time job, but in primary schools a class teacher usually takes on the role.

- Subject Coordinator. Each subject that is taught within the National Curriculum has a subject coordinator responsible for ensuring the effective delivery of it across the school, who may help teachers plan lessons and buy resources for the subject.

- Educational Psychologist. Every school has links to an educational psychologist who helps the school assess and support children with SEN.

- Educational Welfare Officer or Learning Mentor. Not necessarily a teacher, although often a former teacher. Learning Mentors help children experiencing problems, for whatever reason, to get the best out of their education. So they may have a regular counselling session with a child or visit old pupils at their secondary school.

INSET days

INSET stands for in service training. An INSET day means a day in term time – usually towards the beginning or end – when the school closes to pupils so that teachers can catch up on plans to introduce a new initiative, familiarize themselves with new resources or discuss teaching strategies.

For parents, this can be a troublesome part of the school calendar leaving you casting around for childcare or taking valuable holidays off work. Schools are allowed five INSET days a year, and although they are inconvenient for parents they are an invaluable time for teachers trying to keep up to speed with new initiatives and policies in education.

From time to time teachers will also undertake extra training in specific areas, which could mean they are absent from school for anything from a day to a week. These should be welcomed by parents as it shows the teacher is motivated and interested in developing his teaching skills.

Classroom management

Any parent who has hosted a children's party knows only too well that keeping control of a couple of dozen children is up there with Olympic diving in terms of degrees of difficulty.

For the primary schoolteacher, maintaining order in the classroom is a central part of the job and a daily task. Although the classroom environment is quite different to the free-for-all of a kids' party, it's not always a simple matter. Small children are not used to sitting still for long periods, and their concentration can waver. Classroom management – planning the lesson, making sure children have enough to do and at an appropriate level, and making sure the lesson finishes on time – is a fine art.

Managing 30 children is very different to managing one or two. You have to be in command of 30 children and that is almost the first thing that everybody has to learn – how to walk into a classroom and gain 30 children's attention and get them to sit down and listen to what you are talking about. That is the number one skill. Some people are naturals and some people are not and the only thing that helps you do that is practice. And once you've done that, implementing the curriculum and using all your knowledge from the training comes into play. But being able to command the attention of the whole class and getting them to listen to you is still the number one skill.

Julia, trainee teacher and mother of Daniel, 6, and
Jasper, 4.

Most primary schools use a system of positive reinforcement of good behaviour and are careful to make sure all pupils are rewarded. It's easy to praise pupils who are hardworking, well behaved and helpful, but good teachers realize that recognizing improvements in the behaviour of disruptive children is just as important. So a fidgety child might be rewarded for staying seated during a lesson, or a messy child for tidying up after an activity. Teachers also share out simple duties such as taking the register back to the school office or feeding the class hamster in order to encourage a sense of responsibility and care.

Children will often come home from nursery with a smiley sticker on their shirt or a colourful stamp on their hand, rewards for anything from singing nicely to going to the toilet. Later on in school, pupils may be assigned to teams or houses to foster a sense of community, and good behaviour or work will earn team points. Individual rewards might include things like merit badges, or special awards. Outstanding work or improvements in behaviour might be acknowledged with a letter home or a presentation in assembly. Some schools have introduced the concept of 'golden time', whereby children earn time to do some of their favourite things – such as playing games, painting, baking or using the computer – on a Friday afternoon if all week they have been well behaved or worked hard.

These kind of incentives are enjoyed by children and have been shown to have an extremely positive effect on behaviour and motivation.

Circle Time

You might hear your child or their teacher refer to Circle Time, and wonder why the sudden interest in geometry. But what they are talking about is a relatively new method of increasing communication and support between pupils and teachers which has been so successful it is now practised in most primary schools and in an increasing number of secondaries. Circle Time for schools was devised and popularized by a teacher, Jenny Mosley, but it is based on a model that has been in use in other settings, such as industry and counselling, since the 1960s.

At regular (usually weekly) Circle Time sessions, pupils and their teachers sit in a circle and discuss problems or issues that affect them. There are several rules such as no interrupting – among younger children a toy might be passed round and only the person holding it is allowed to speak – and no criticism. Children are encouraged to speak openly and honestly and to bring up any worries or concerns they have so that the rest of the class can suggest solutions.

But Circle Time is more than just having a chat. The subjects discussed at Circle Time might include sensitive issues such as bullying or making friends, so they need to be carefully handled and teachers should have some training before they start using it.

Circle Time can improve listening and communication skills as well as fostering a sense of trust and belonging between pupils. Complementary sessions such as philosophy for children and thinking skills are becoming more commonplace in schools as they look for creative and enjoyable ways of improving pupil learning and behaviour. Some schools with a history of discipline problems have found it little short of revolutionary in promoting a positive ethos.

NINE

Special Needs

One in five children in England and Wales is classified as having Special Educational Needs (SEN) at some time or other. These can range from something like needing extra help with reading to severe physical disabilities. It simply means that your child requires extra assistance with their schooling.

The Department for Education and Skills definition includes:

- difficulties with reading, writing, speaking or maths
- physical disabilities
- problems with sight, hearing or speech
- mental disabilities
- emotional or behavioural problems
- medical or health conditions.

SEN does not cover the possible language difficulties of children for whom English is not their mother tongue – although they may receive special help at school. More controversially, perhaps, gifted children are not regarded as having SEN either, for reasons that are explained later in this chapter.

If your child has special needs it is important to know what your and your child's rights are, what help is available and how to ensure that all your child's educational needs are being met. The world of SEN can be confusing to the newcomer, full of acronyms, jargon and complex assessments and forms of tuition. More than any other area of education, it is the one parents need to continually struggle against, mainly because of financial constraints. The good news is that your child has rights to an education that takes her special needs into account and compensates for them.

A bit of background

Knowledge of special needs and the help available has improved dramatically in recent years. The term 'Special Educational Needs' was introduced by the 1981 Education Act and replaced a raft of other terms that had not been changed since the 1944 Education Act. Numerous disorders have been discovered since then and our knowledge of others has increased. Terms like 'educationally sub-normal', 'remedial' and 'retarded' are obsolete, as is the attitude that there is 'something wrong' with your child.

The increased understanding of different learning styles has also had an effect on the way children with special needs are taught. Although much more needs to be done to include the theory of MI (Multiple Intelligences) in teacher training, the recognition of more than one way of learning and teaching has made the system more accommodating to the needs of all children.

Inclusion

Just as the medical profession's understanding of different behaviours and disorders has deepened, so society's attitude has become more enlightened. Years ago, the vast majority of children with physical or mental disabilities were educated in special schools. There were (and still are) schools for the blind, the deaf, for children with behavioural problems, and for those with dyslexia. Nowadays this kind of 'segregation' is not always thought appropriate and, where possible, the emphasis is on inclusive education: in other words, mainstream schools accommodating the needs of children with SEN.

Since 1992, the proportion of children with statements (more serious long-term SEN) who are educated in mainstream schools has risen from 40 to 55 per cent. As inclusion gathers pace and more and more special schools are closed or amalgamated. These closures seem to have stopped in the last few years, as the rise in numbers of children with autism and behavioural problems means specialist settings are back on the agenda for some pupils. It is up to your LEA to decide whether they will fund a place for your child in a special school if that is what you want.

Deciding whether a child is better off in a mainstream school or not is going to depend on the child and the nature of their special educational need. In practice, while the legislative framework for inclusion may be willing, the practical availability of provision may be weak in your area. There are wide variations in the way local authorities deal with special needs education. In the London Borough of Newham, for example, in 2001 8.8 per cent of children with statements were in special schools, while in Liverpool for the same year the figure was 66.8 per cent.

Recent legislation has provided fresh impetus for the movement for inclusive education for children with physical disabilities. The 2002 Special Educational Needs and Disability Act makes it illegal to treat a disabled person 'less favourably' than a non-disabled person because of their disability. If the disabled person is found to be at a 'substantial disadvantage' compared with other students then schools have to take steps to rectify this, whether this be through the provision of support workers or changes to the building or teaching styles.

The rights of a child with SEN in a mainstream school are set out in a 'code of practice' under the 1993 Education Act, which explains the protocol for identifying, assessing and meeting special educational needs. It was updated in 2001 and is the framework to which LEAs, schools and all bodies working in the world of SEN and education work. The code of practice is the best place to start for an insight into the obligations and responsibilities that your school and LEA have towards your child. It can be downloaded from the DfES website or you can request a hard copy from your LEA.

This is the way the code works. There are three stages by which your child is assessed:

- First, **school action** is taken by a teacher nominated as Special Educational Needs Coordinator (SENCO) when a problem is identified.
- Second, **school action plus** is when professional help is usually brought in.
- Third, **statementing** occurs, which involves a full statement of SEN.

Identifying a special educational need

Your child's SEN may be obvious to you and be something you knew about before they even started school. Alternatively, it may be something that an outside professional such as a teacher, doctor or health visitor has identified. In either case, recognizing and classifying a special need early on is always important, and children in nurseries and playgroups in England are routinely assessed so see whether they have learning difficulties. These assessments will feed into the Foundation Stage Profile made when children start school to identify and tackle problems as early as possible.

Often the first hurdle for many parents is to get a teacher or school to recognize that a child does have special needs, as not all teachers recognize that parents know their child best. You may be told that problems will sort themselves out. Conversely some parents can find it very difficult to accept that their child has special educational needs, and will fight the school's assessment and provision for their child.

Elliot behaved in a very odd way as a baby but it wasn't odd to anybody else, it was just lots of little things really. And other people would say, 'Well my child does that' and make light of it, which people do, but I think if you have a gut feeling about your child's behaviour you should really go with your feeling rather than being put off by common-sense advice. My feeling was always there and my feeling was right.
Louise, mother of Elliot 9, Noah, 8, and Kitty, 3.

Once SEN have been identified a process is set on course with the child being assessed to decide what special educational needs they have and how they can be helped. How and when parents find out that their child is receiving additional help can be haphazard. Ideally they will receive written notification or have a private conversation with a member of staff, although sometimes they might find out through a less considered casual conversation in the playground or an overheard remark made by another child.

An Individual Education Plan (IEP) will be produced, identifying the SEN (which could simply be difficulty in learning to read) and outlining targets and strategies to support learning. This is usually completed by the teacher in consultation with the school's Special Educational Needs Coordinator (SENCO). For as long as a child is on the register he will have an IEP, which is reviewed annually. As a parent you have every right to see the IEP and should, ideally, be involved in drawing it up and commenting on it.

Every school has a SENCO. In large schools this will be their only job, while in smaller ones it will be an additional duty. A SENCO is the teacher responsible for ensuring that children identified as having SEN are getting the appropriate support in the school. Their responsibilities also include drawing up the Individual Education Plans and liaising with any external agencies. They are also good to talk to about things you can do at home that will help with your child's school life.

Once your child has had a special education need identified, he will go on the school's Special Needs Register and stays there for as long as he needs special attention – this could be for as little as a term or for the rest of their school careers, depending on the need.

Individual education plans

I understand it's very scary for parents when you are contacted by a school and you're told they want to place your child on the Special Needs Register. But you aren't allowed to put a child on a special needs register just for normal classroom differentiation, you have to be needing to do something above and beyond what normally happens in the classroom in order to put the child on the Special Needs Register.

What I say to parents is, 'This makes the school accountable to you'. The school is, through the Individual Education Plan, formalizing and putting down on paper the extra help that the school is giving your child. Usually it's already happening.

It's not that your child is – to put it in terribly blunt terms – 'thick', and I think parents worry that that's what it means. It doesn't. It means that we need to do something extra for them. It just makes sure the school is responding to your individual child's needs.

Kate, deputy headteacher and mother of Eliza, 6.

There are as many Individual Education Plans as there are children with special needs. Each one is drawn up with the intention of helping that child receive the best education possible; whether his difficulties are large or small. For example, a child with temporary hearing loss due to glue ear may have an IEP outlining some simple steps that can be taken until their problem is resolved, such as sitting him at the front of the class, tapping him on the shoulder to get his attention and tactics to ensure good eye contact.

For children with more severe disabilities or behavioural problems, an IEP will be the first of several documents charting a course to help them through school. Along the way children such as these will need the support of a Learning Support Assistant (LSA), a person employed to provide in-school support for pupils with SEN and/or disabilities.

The IEP should provide answers to the following questions:

■ What is the SEN? Precise diagnosis is not always possible and may change over time.

■ How is the school going to deal with it? Is there additional outside help that could be accessed? Many LEAs have outreach staff.

■ If specialist staff are going to be involved, what are their qualifications? Children with special educational needs are often given help either by classroom assistants or teachers with no specialist knowledge or training in SEN.

■ What targets have been set for your child?

■ When are those targets going to be reviewed?

IEPs are usually signed by parents. But before you do, it is a good idea to take the IEP home and read it through to check if all areas have been covered and that it addresses all your areas of concern. If you have any questions, make a note of them and ask the SENCO. Ask for clarification of any aspect of it that is unclear to you. There is a lot of jargon used in educational and medical fields so there is no shame in asking exactly what things mean.

Every year there is a review of the IEP, and you should prepare for this by making a list of points you want to make to the SENCO or classteacher. These can be very emotionally demanding sessions as what is being discussed is what your child is not very good at. It is a good idea to take a partner or friend along for support and to take notes of what is said. You may also want to highlight the areas your child excels in and ask how these are going to be used to further his progress.

Statements

Children with more serious ongoing problems have a 'statement' (or 'record of needs' as it is known in Scotland), which is a statutory record of what your child's educational needs are and the provision that the LEA thinks is appropriate. 'Statementing' is fairly uncommon and used in a minority of children with special needs – one in five children has SEN, but only one in thirty has a statement.

The statement of SEN records:

Part 1: Personal details

Part 2: The child's needs

Part 3: Provision (how to meet those needs)

Part 4: Placement (school)

Part 5: Any non-educational needs your child has

Part 6: How these non-educational needs will be met

This process does not take place without registering your views on each stage of it. You can have a 'named person' to give you support and help you express your views. This could be a friend, a professional such as a doctor, or someone from a voluntary organization. It could also be an officer from your LEA's parent partnership office. Every local authority has parent-partnership officers who are meant to be independent sources of advice and information to parents and carers of children with SEN. You can get a number from your local education authority department.

Recent legislation has given headteachers, and parents, the right to ask the LEA to produce a statement of needs.

Although the legislative framework looks impressive, what happens in practice may be far from ideal. In many areas, for example, there is a two-year waiting period for the statementing process to happen. An Audit Commission Report on Special Educational Needs published in December 2002 found that:

- Early intervention can make a difference but has yet to become the norm.

- Arrangements for funding SEN provision in early years settings remain 'incoherent and piecemeal'.

- Parents of children with SEN often have difficulty with school admissions. More than two-thirds of children with statements are educated in mainstream schools, but many parents feel there is a lack of suitable provision locally and an unwelcoming attitude in some schools.

- Children with SEN are sometimes denied access to certain lessons, extra-curricular activities and social opportunities. They are much more likely to be permanently excluded.

- National targets and performance tables don't reflect the achievements of children with SEN – so inclusive schools may appear to perform badly. This can make schools less welcoming of children with special needs.

What if you disagree with your LEA?

If you do want to challenge your LEA's decision on your child, then the body that decides unresolved disputes (in England and Wales) is the Special Educational Needs and Disability Tribunal. The powers of the tribunal are quite wide ranging:

■ It can force the LEA to make an assessment of SEN if you or the school believes one is necessary and the LEA has refused to do so. It cannot, however, tell the LEA what should go into any statement.

■ If a statement has already been done it can order changes to Parts 2 (needs), 3 (Provision) and 4 (Placement).

■ The Tribunal now deals with Disability Discrimination appeals. If it decides that a child has been discriminated against because of his disability it can order action to put right the effect of that discrimination (but not financial compensation).

The Tribunal's decision is binding on the LEA and although the Lord Chancellor appoints its president and chairman and the Secretary of State for Education and Employment appoints its members, it is otherwise independent of the government. If you disagree with the Tribunal's decision then you can appeal to the High Court, but only if you think it made a legal mistake and not just because you are unhappy with the decision. You could also try contacting your local MP and enlisting his or her support.

Whether you are taking things as far as an appeal or simply writing to the school to request an assessment, there are some tips as to how you can put the best case:

■ List your child's difficulties both at home and at school, but also point out your child's strengths and areas of intelligence so that these can be used to further his learning.

■ Details are important, whether they relate to something academic, social or just personal to him.

■ Keep records of all meetings – dates and who was present at them. Don't throw away any letters or information you have been sent.

■ Remember you know your child better than anyone else.

There is a distinct lack of research into the link between SEN and educational achievements. Some conditions deemed special educational needs are not by any means an indicator of lack of intelligence or underachievement. Many people with dyslexia, for example, have had extremely successful professional lives and there is evidence to suggest dyslexia actually enhances visual and spatial awareness – hence the high number of artists with dyslexia. The Audit Commission's 2002 report found that little is known about how well children with SEN achieve in school because of poor monitoring by schools and LEAs. There are, for example, no figures as to what are the most common diagnostic special educational needs at primary school.

Most SEN are on a spectrum and will need differing degrees of help. Many commonly overlap – for example, dyslexia and dyspraxia. What follows is a list of the most common diagnostic special educational needs.

Physical disabilities

There is such a wide variety of physical disabilities that any real analysis may not be very useful. Legally, since the 2002 Special Educational Needs and Disability Act it is illegal to treat a disabled person less favourably than an able-bodied person for a reason that relates to the disability. Schools will, therefore, have to become more inclusive of children with physical disabilities, as long as this does not impact too negatively on the interests of the rest of the school population.

Dyslexia

Dyslexia is a neurological disorder that affects a person's ability to process language. Typically, people with dyslexia will have trouble learning to read, write and spell, but they may also find it difficult to remember things and to think sequentially. In Britain's schools 350,000 children are diagnosed dyslexic – on average one child in every class.

Early intervention and help at school is vital and there are various tools and tests that help diagnose dyslexia, although there is no simple diagnostic test. Certain behavioural traits may indicate dyslexia in a child, for example, putting clothes on the wrong way round or the inability to distinguish between left and right or to learn simple rhymes. There may be a tendency to spoonerisms (e.g. par cark), spelling the same word differently, confusing words (e.g. dog for god) and overall poor literacy skills. These, of course, are common in all young children but most will grow out of them by the age of 7.

Outward signs of dyslexia in older primary-aged children may include difficulties in copying notes from the board, interpreting written instructions, organizing work or remembering passages of text, erratic spelling or poor handwriting. General practical rules for teachers and parents include:

- Writing instructions on homework and things to remember for school in a notebook.

- Presenting information in non-written forms wherever possible, using instead symbols, graphs, pictures, charts and tapes.

- Developing computer skills can help dyslexic children as they usually find typing easier than writing.

Autism

Although it was first identified in the 1940s, science is still a long way off fully understanding autism: its causes are unknown and there is no real diagnostic test. People with autism will have difficulty with social interaction, communication and imagination. They have a tendency to repetitive, obsessive behaviour and a dislike of changes in routine. A recent report for the Medical Research Council reckons that six in every 1,000 young children have a disorder within the spectrum of autism.

Like many behavioural problems, autism varies greatly in its effects. At the 'higher functioning' end of the spectrum, Asperger's syndrome is a form of autism in which a child may have language skills and average or above-average intelligence but will find social interaction and relationships awkward. Children with Asperger's syndrome are more likely to attend a mainstream school than children with autism.

Autism is usually, but not always, spotted before a child reaches school age. Once diagnosed the LEA will decide whether the child should go to a special school or not.

General rules for autistic children in a mainstream school include:

- Ensuring staff members (in addition to the child's teacher and SENCO) understand the condition.

- Making special arrangements for playtime as autistic children may prefer to spend them alone or with one other person – a 'buddy' system can be helpful.
- Teachers should continually check that instructions and teaching have been understood.
- Teacher and parent should liaise about any planned changes to the child's routine as they can be very upsetting to autistic children and should be avoided if possible.

Down's Syndrome

There are about 600 children born each year with Down's Syndrome, many fewer than there used to be because of the use of ante-natal scans in detecting the syndrome. There are numerous medical problems associated with the condition but in terms of education, children with Down's Syndrome will have some degree of difficulty in areas of speech and language, hearing, reading, writing and social skills.

While the 1944 Education Act innaccurately deemed children with Down's Syndrome as 'ineducable' the move towards inclusion means that many more are now in mainstream schools. Children with Down's Syndrome will need extra support in a school setting, such as speech and language therapy and practical help with schoolwork. Research has shown, however, that given the right support children with Down's Syndrome can do very well in a mainstream school.

Attention Deficiency Disorder (ADD) and Attention Deficit Hyperactivity Disorder (ADHD)

ADD and ADHD – the commonly used term for what is officially called hyperkinetic disorder – affect about five in every 100 primary school children. The cause of ADD is not known but as it often runs in families, genetic factors seem to play a large part. As with many of these disorders it affects boys more than girls, and again there is no diagnostic test.

Children with ADD and ADHD will be restless and overactive, prone to chattering and interrupting people, easily distracted and unable to wait their turn. They may also behave impulsively, and appear clumsy, fidgety and disorganized.

Most children with ADD are of normal intelligence but they may have been slow learning to talk, find reading hard and have difficulties making friends. Their problems and frustrations often contribute to their behavioural problems.

At school all teachers should be made aware of the problems associated with ADD. It often results in low self-esteem, so children with ADD need extra attention, lots of encouragement and carefully structured activities.

Medication will not cure ADD/ADHD, but it can be used to create a period when a child can learn and practise new skills. A good doctor will always give a 'drug holiday', a period when the child is not prescribed any drugs.

Emotional and behavioural difficulties (EBD)

This is a broad term that covers a range of issues, from children who might be called 'naughty' and lacking in discipline to those with a specific mental disorder. The Office for National Statistics estimates that around one in ten children has a mental disorder, which could be linked to things like bereavement, trauma, depression, an eating disorder or physical and sexual abuse.

There is a shortage of educational psychologists to address the needs of children with EBD so they are often the subject of exclusions or taught in Pupil Referral Units – a kind of halfway house for children at risk of exclusion. Other options include learning or behavioural support units which provide extra help, usually within the school setting.

The Government's Behaviour Improvement Programme targets children and schools with behaviour management problems and gives them access to the services of BESTS – Behaviour and Educational Support Teams. These teams include health professionals such as psychologists and educational experts to provide tailor-made support for children and their families. They also provide support for the school in initiating and maintaining behaviour policies.

Dyspraxia

Dyspraxia is a neurological condition that can be present on its own but is commonly associated with dyslexia. About 6 per cent of the population has dyspraxia, and boys are four times more likely to have it than girls. In each class it is likely that there will be one child with dyspraxia.

Symptoms are evident from an early age although the cause is often not identified. Babies with dyspraxia are usually irritable and hard to comfort. They are slow to reach developmental milestones, and often prefer the 'bottom shuffle' to learning to crawl.

Between the ages of three and five children with dyspraxia typically bump into things and fall over more than other children, have poor fine motor skills in general and avoid constructional toys like jigsaws. They will have continued messy eating, limited creative play and left- or right-handedness may be yet to be established. They can be very sensitive to sensory stimulation, including high levels of noise.

At primary school, they may have difficulty in PE lessons, be slow at dressing and be unable to tie shoe laces. Writing and drawing can be a problem, so copying things down becomes difficult.

People with dyspraxia often have above average intelligence and with the right encouragement and support can do well at school. Things that can help include:

- Breaking tasks down into a simple and logical sequence.
- Repeating reminders of the tasks and the steps necessary to achieving it.
- Minimizing distractions while working.
- Using a triangular pen or pencil if handwriting is a problem.

Homework

We look at different learning styles all the time with children with special needs. I run a special homework programme for children with dyslexia in the school. Children at Key Stage 2 are given a text and questions. The first thing they have to do with the text is to chop it up into pieces and actually stick it onto a different piece of paper. So the whole idea of them physically moving the text helps them to get into it – they are breaking it down into bite-sized chunks. We talk about colour coding. So they look at question one – we don't ask them to write the questions down – and they think 'I'm going to answer Q1 in red' and then they highlight the place in the text that answers Q1. So it's using a multi-sensory approach to develop learning.

Kate, deputy headteacher and mother of Eliza, 6

It is important that a child with SEN gets good quality homework that is at a level and presented in a way that is appropriate. If you are unsure about this, talk to the teacher or the SENCO to make sure your child's special needs are being considered.

Transport

LEAs are generally under a duty to provide free transport to a child's nearest suitable school provided that it is beyond the statutory walking distance of his home (two miles for children under 8 and three miles for those over 8). What is a suitable school for a child with SEN may well be different to that of a child without SEN or a statement, but the principle is the same. If the parents have chosen a school that is not what the LEA considers to be the nearest suitable school then there is no duty to provide free transport. All applications for free transport, spare seats on school buses or help paying for fares should be made to your LEA.

A word about gifted children

Until recently there was no special provision for gifted children, but in 1999 the Government introduced a national programme to improve the identification, education and support of gifted and talented children. This strategy is part of its Excellence in Cities scheme, which directs extra funds to deprived urban areas.

The 'Gifted and Talented' programme targets children who are especially able in more than one subject but are underachieving. Gifted children may hide their abilities for fear of being singled out and so become reticent in class and difficult to involve. Bullying is often an issue for gifted children, so sometimes problems at school and their need for individual attention means that parents decide to educate them at home.

Characteristics of gifted children include some, although not all, of the following:

- talking and reading early and developing a wide vocabulary
- a very good memory and being able to retain information
- being extremely curious and able to concentrate for long periods on subjects of interest
- having an unusual and vivid imagination
- showing strong feelings and opinions and having an odd sense of humour.

Tips for getting the best out of the system, whatever your child's special needs

All sorts of school issues can impact more heavily on children with SEN. Figures show, for example, that children with special needs are three times more likely to be excluded than other children. This involves more work for you as a parent in terms of keeping on top of their progress and becoming aware of difficulties before they become a problem. But remember the system is there to serve your child.

- Join a parent organization. There are many organizations for parents of children with general and specific SEN, and they can be a useful source of information and support.
- Develop a good partnership with the school. You are part of a team and should share any relevant information. Your observations can be a valuable part of ensuring progress.
- Before any kind of meeting write down a list of your questions, as it is easy to forget.

- Keep records of meetings including dates and who was present. Any letters and information you are sent should be kept for reference.

- Do not forget the importance of your child being involved in all aspects of the school's activities and extra-curricular events.

- It can be intimidating dealing with educational, medical and psychological professionals, but don't be afraid to ask if you are not sure what certain words or terms mean.

- Remember you know your child best. Don't underestimate your knowledge as a parent.

- Do not just focus on the difficulties and weaknesses of your child. All children are intelligent in different ways. Keep pointing out your child's strengths and areas of intelligence so they can be used to help his learning.

TEN

School Life

Your child, her school and you as a parent are involved in a complex relationship of rights and responsibilities. Many of these, such as the right to an education and the right of appeal against an exclusion, are enshrined in law. Others, such as the right to be consulted on school policy on bullying are not statutory as such, but are governed by protocol and various government guidelines. Perhaps the most important duty of a school is that it has a 'duty of care' towards your child. This means it is responsible 'in loco parentis' for her safety and well-being.

Since 1998, all schools have had to produce a home-school agreement setting out the school's aims, values and responsibilities towards its pupils. A home-school agreement also states what the responsibilities of the child's parents are, and what the school expects of its pupils. Parents do not have to sign this agreement and it does not have any standing in law, but it does tell you where the school stands with regard to things like behaviour, attendance and pastoral care. As well as the home-school agreement schools are expected to produce various other policy statements – on discipline, bullying and child protection – which should be available to the parents.

This chapter aims to put these rules and regulations into perspective and make them easier to understand.

School uniform

There is no uniform at my daughter's school and woe betide anyone who tries to remotely suggest to the headteacher that there should be one. She believes that children should be individuals and not dressed in the same clothes. It would be easier for me and I actually think it gives a nice sense of belonging if children have a recognizable uniform. Imogen would really like a uniform. When we get dressed in the morning she says 'Do these clothes look like a uniform?' – you know, flowered skirt, flowered top and stripy tights! I am pro-uniform although I don't feel strongly about it.

Louise, mother of Imogen, 6.

The first school rule you need to know about, before your child even sets foot in school, is its uniform policy. School uniforms – virtually mandatory in the post-war years and then widely abandoned in the 1960s and 1970s – have been making something of a comeback recently.

A school's governing body decides on its uniform policy. Uniforms are more common at secondary schools than primary schools, and can vary from a simple sweatshirt with logo to the full shirt and tie, blazer and cap.

Opinion varies over whether uniform is a good thing or not – a recent DfES survey showed that 89 per cent of parents were in favour of uniforms and that most believe they improve academic performance and discipline.

Price is an important factor. In 2001, an average primary school uniform (including a sports kit) cost £92 for girls and £115 for boys. There is no statutory help for poorer parents, the number of LEAs that does give discretionary grants to help cover the cost is declining, and the grants themselves are nowhere near enough to cover the cost.

The DfES has addressed complaints about expensive uniforms by issuing guidelines to governing bodies saying that they should not 'be so expensive as to leave pupils or their families feeling socially excluded' and that the governing body should be 'receptive to any reasonable complaint' about their uniform policy. The guidelines also say that non-compliance on the grounds of religion, race or culture, for instance the wearing of headscarves, should not be punished.

The Equal Opportunities Commission have threatened court action over cases of girls wanting to wear trousers in schools where the uniform policy stipulates a skirt, but these have so far been settled out of court. Uniform disputes are rare in primary school, and generally speaking younger children are quite happy wearing a uniform as a badge of their belonging.

School attendance and truancy

While figures for truanting at secondary school have remained stable over the years, the problem is worsening at primary level. In some areas, a third of the pupils picked up by truancy sweeps were under 11. Research has shown that the most persistent truants at secondary schools started skipping lessons in their primary school.

A 2003 study of more than 600 primary school children found that 27 per cent had skipped classes – usually because of bullying, dislike of a teacher or to avoid a test.

Another worry for schools is the fact that many of these children were with their parents when they were picked up. If parents appear to be condoning their children's truancy it makes the job of enforcing attendance even more difficult for schools.

There are various reasons why the government takes truanting seriously. There is an obvious connection with academic underachievement: a 1998 study found that one in three regular truants fail to achieve any GCSE passes. The link between truancy and crime is also well established: two thirds of truants have committed a crime, and five per cent of all crimes are committed by truants during school hours. In schools where truancy is a problem, catering for occasional attenders or reintegrating truants can disrupt the progress of all children. The government's line is that 'if you are not in school you are not learning'.

Localized truancy sweeps by police and education welfare officers have been stepped up to deal with the problem. Legal measures may be used, including increased fines of up to £2,500 and, most controversially, prison sentences for parents of persistent truants. By law the parent is responsible for their child's attendance at school, and in 2002 Patricia Amos became the first parent to be jailed – for 60 days – because two of her children had such poor attendance rates.

A prison sentence is obviously a last resort, and most LEAs realize that prosecution is not always the best course of action. A new, fast track legal process piloted in some parts of the country in 2003 gave parents of truants 12 weeks – about one term – to improve their child's performance or face court action. In more than half the cases their attendance improved.

Schools have to produce attendance figures in their annual report and in league tables. Any truancy is described as 'unauthorized absence'. Schools require letters from parents or a phone call to the school office to authorize any absence from school because of illness, hospital appointments, and so on. This figure is recorded separately.

The practice of taking children out of school during term time to take advantage of cheaper holidays has become widespread. Ministers have criticized this 'middle-class truancy' as losing valuable learning time. And while schools have the discretion to grant up to 10 days a year for holidays during term-time, it is certainly not guaranteed that your headteacher will allow it. Depending on their policy, they may look favourably on family reasons or the educational opportunities of such a trip.

Exclusions

> I feel that the lack of discipline in schools is really what's affecting our present day society. I think children need a structure in their lives and that is what they are missing. So I'd rather my child went to a school where there was a structure so at least what you are implementing at home is being reinforced and the child doesn't get confused.
>
> Rodney, father of Jesil, 6, and Elai, 3.

Persistent truancy is not among the list of things that will get your child excluded. In fact, the government's guidelines state that exclusion should only be used as a last resort and when there has been a serious breach of the school's discipline policy. Truancy, lateness, not handing homework in, uniform transgressions, and so on do not warrant exclusion.

Despite the government's efforts to reduce school exclusions they have risen continually over recent years. In 1990–91 there were 2,910 permanent exclusions, but by 1997 that figure had risen to 12,700. The figures for 2000–01 showed an 11 per cent increase. Most of these are from secondary schools, but 1,460 children were excluded from primary schools in England.

There are two types of exclusion – permanent exclusion, and fixed-period exclusions for a period of up to 45 days in a school year. The government guidelines say that fixed-period exclusions should be of the shortest time necessary and that if the exclusion lasts for more than a day schoolwork should be set and marked. Indefinite exclusions are not lawful.

There are two main grounds for exclusion: either a serious breach of the school's behaviour policy or because allowing the pupil to remain in school would seriously harm the education or welfare of that pupil or others in the school. The only person who has the power to exclude children is the headteacher or the acting head. All exclusions have to be recorded and if a child is excluded for more than five days in one term, or at a time that means she misses a public examination, then the discipline committee of the governing body of the school must be informed. If this happens then you have the right to put your case in person to the governing body. It is good practice for governing bodies to meet with you even if the exclusion is for less than five days, but at the very least you have the right to put your case in writing.

The governor's discipline committee has to review all permanent exclusions by law and decide whether they support the headteacher's decision or not. If they do not agree that all other alternatives have been tried then the child can be 'reinstated'.

When a child is excluded the school must inform the parents in writing of the length of the exclusion and the reasons for it. If the headteacher thinks an offence has been committed then they can exclude a child while the incident is investigated, and an appropriate adult should be present if children are being questioned.

Many more boys than girls are excluded, and the most common reasons given are verbal abuse of a member of staff (either on or off the school premises) and 'threatening others with intended or actual physical harm', which would include bullying. Certain children have been identified as being at greatest risk of exclusion – among them children with SEN, children in care, African-Caribbean boys, and children who have just started school. If your child is from one of these groups schools should be giving her extra support, and you may be able to use this fact to overturn the exclusion.

For detailed advice on exclusions, The Advisory Centre for Education is an independent advice centre for parents (details are at the back of the book).

Smacking

A smack on the hand or backside with a cane or plimsoll used to be par for the course in Britain's schools. Headteachers routinely dished out six of the best for misbehaviour – but such punishments are now consigned to history.

Smacking was outlawed in UK state schools in 1986 and in independent schools in 1998. But the issue of whether children should be subject to corporal punishment has not gone away. While children's charities have campaigned for smacking a child to be made illegal, and appealed to parents who hit their children to stop, some schools have attempted to reintroduce smacking as a form of punishment for bad behaviour.

In 1999, the European Court of Human Rights ruled that there was nothing to stop schools smacking their children if parents agreed to it, and in the following year, an attempt by a group of Christian schools to claim a Biblical mandate for smacking failed in the High Court. The school's case was based on the line from the Book of Proverbs: 'Folly is bound up in the heart of a child, but the rod of discipline will drive it far from him.'

Countless studies have shown that smacking does not work as a form of behaviour control: it merely fuels resentment, can be psychologically damaging and makes children more likely to use violence themselves.

However, a survey by the *Times Educational Supplement* found that a significant number of parents want to see it reintroduced into schools – 51 per cent were in favour and 47 per cent against.

But this is unlikely to happen. In 2003, childminders were banned from disciplining children in their care – previously they had been allowed, with the agreement of parents, to use 'reasonable chastisement.' The government has, however, shied away so far from an outright ban on smacking.

The flipside of this legislation has been that, as behaviour in some schools has deteriorated, several teachers have faced court action after they have allegedly used force to break up fights or to keep discipline.

Pupil referral units

Pupil Referral Units (PRUs) are run by LEAs to provide education for children who, for whatever reason, do not attend mainstream schools. This could include children who have been excluded, teenage mothers, children who are school phobic or pupils being assessed for a statement of SEN. Because they are smaller than schools and have a rapidly changing pupil roll, PRUs are not subject to all the same legislative requirements that apply to mainstream schools and special schools. They differ from mainstream schools in a number of ways, the most important being:

- They are smaller than ordinary schools, with a pupil to staff ratio of about five to one.
- They are run by a management committee rather than a board of governors, which might be made up of headteachers from mainstream schools and representatives from social services, probation, parents and others.
- Because their pupil roll changes frequently, they do not need to teach the full National Curriculum.

School trips

School trips can be a memorable, enjoyable and highly educational part of the learning process. They help children and teachers bond with each other, and build confidence and social skills in children.

Most trips will be in the form of a local outing to a museum, theme park or countryside attraction, but many primary schools take older children on trips further afield lasting up to a week, perhaps to an outdoor centre, a seaside resort or even abroad. At secondary school the trips become still more adventurous – and expensive.

On average, children will go on at least two school trips a year – equivalent to some 20 million days out. Though the majority of these pass without incident, there have been several high-profile tragedies where, because of inadequate supervision, children's lives have been lost. In 1993, four sixth-formers died while canoeing in Lyme Bay, Dorset. The director of the activity centre was convicted of manslaughter and the regulations governing school trips were tightened up by the Activity Centres (Young Person's Safety) Act the following year.

This legislation set up the Adventure Activities Licensing Authority, which has the job of monitoring and licensing activity centres in the UK. Because of limited resources it is only responsible for licensing centres which offer a range of what is classified as the most dangerous activities – this includes climbing and sailing but not including swimming or walking.

Despite the greater security measures in place, fatal accidents continue to happen, but the risk involved in school trips is still relatively low – fewer than 50 children have died on school trips in the last 20 years but 200 die on Britain's roads every year. Properly supervised, school trips can provide some of the most inspiring experiences of childhood.

The guidelines on school trips include the following:

- Parents should have enough written information on the visit to be able to make an informed decision on whether they want their child to go.

- Schools are legally required to carry out a risk assessment noting any places or times on the planned trip where children may be in danger. The school must do what is 'reasonably practicable' to avoid risks.

■ Teachers should have visited the site previously so they can use first-hand experience. Many of the locations for trips will have education officers who will help them do the assessment, and increasingly teachers are trained to carry out these assessments properly.

The ratio of teachers to pupils on a school trip depends on the age group, activity and location. For a low-risk trip – to a museum or a walk – the following is suggested:

■ One adult for every six pupils in Years 1–3 (reception classes should have a higher ratio).

■ One adult for every 10–15 pupils in Years 4–5.

■ One adult for every 15–20 pupils in Year 7 and upwards.

If your child is going on a school trip, especially one involving adventure activities, then do not be afraid to ask questions about what she will be doing. Make sure you know the kind of activities they have planned and the clothing or equipment they need. Check departure and return dates and times.

You do not have to send your child on any school trip although it is often expected that you will, and if you don't then it presents the school with an administrative headache and of course your child will be disappointed. On residential trips the headteacher is allowed to charge parents for board and lodging as well as the full costs if the trip is regarded as on 'optional extra' – i.e. wholly or mainly outside school hours or not part of the National Curriculum. Depending on your LEA and school you may get board and lodging paid for if you are on benefits and the trip is not regarded as an optional extra.

Legally the education that is provided wholly or mainly during school hours is free, so headteachers cannot impose a charge on parents if the trip takes place in school hours. In practice, parents are usually asked for a specific amount as a voluntary contribution. The guidelines state that if parents do not make a contribution their children should not be discriminated against. Often schools have a fund which they use to help less well-off parents pay for trips.

School dinners

The main thing I would change about school is the lunch. For school lunch they do give you salads sometimes, but they also give you fatty things like burgers and chips and I don't really like it. I want to eat more healthily.

Kiana, 9.

The arrangements for school meals – and their quality – vary greatly from school to school. When, as education minister, Margaret Thatcher famously stopped free school milk, nutritional guidelines for school meals were also abolished. Local authorities were forced to choose the most competitive catering services on offer and private companies took over from LEA school dinner services in providing food to most of the nation's schools. Schools were allowed to opt out of borough-wide catering arrangements in 2000, and nutritional guidelines were reintroduced the following year. Some schools have made great improvements to the food they serve up, but a survey by the organic food campaign group The Soil Association found that some schools spend as little as 35p on school dinners – less than the cost of a prison meal. Because of concern over links between additives in food and hyperactivity, some schools have begun serving more nutritious dinners.

Dinners

For years, the children at St Peter's primary school in East Bridgford, Nottinghamshire, had got used to processed and pre-prepared food, and catering manager Jeanette Orrey's job involved little more than serving it up.

But when the school decided to take control of its own school meals in 2000, that all changed. Now nearly all the food comes from local suppliers, much of it is organic and meals are freshly made for the same cost per head – about 70 pence – as other schools in the county. Parents and senior citizens are invited into the school for lunch one day a week and 80 per cent of the children now choose school dinners – before Jeannette took over it was less than half.

Jeanette and her staff have won several awards for their cooking, and she has set up an advisory service (*www.primarychoice.co.uk*) to help other schools do the same.

More than half of Britain's children take packed lunches into school. Although these could provide a healthy alternative to school meals, a recent Food Standards Agency survey of lunchboxes from 24 primary schools found only 21 per cent met the minimum dietary standards required of cooked school dinners, and less than half contained a piece of fresh fruit.

Eligibility for free school dinners is often used as an indication of a school's social intake. Only one in five students is eligible, but the stigma of free school meals (some schools make free-meals pupils wait until paying children have been served) means that every day around 350,000 school lunches go uneaten in UK schools.

Although the government introduced a scheme entitling all children under 7 to free fruit in schools, there is still a long way to providing a healthy school environment. Another issue in school is access to drinking water. Around 10 per cent of pupils have no drinking water facilities in their school, and more than half have to put their mouths around a tap or drink from cupped hands if they want some water.

Physical education

Physical Education is a statutory part of all four key stages of the National Curriculum, and it aims to give pupils a grounding in games, gymnastics, dance, swimming, athletics and outdoor adventure activities. Recent changes to the Curriculum means it now incorporates the use of ICT in PE teaching, with a focus on tactical awareness and decision-making.

In 2002 the Government launched The Physical Education, School Sport and Club Links Strategy to promote sport opportunities for the 5–16 age group. The primary aim of the strategy is to increase the percentage of school children in England who spend a minimum of two hours a week on high quality PE in and out of school to 75 per cent. The pressure of teaching the National Curriculum's core subjects means that subjects like PE and Design Technology suffer, and currently only 25 per cent of schools already spend two hours on PE. New funds have been made available for investing in facilities, staff training and forging closer links between schools and sports clubs.

Following an outcry over the sale of playing fields in the 1980s and 1990s, schools and LEAs now have to get permission from the Education Secretary if they want to sell off their land, and the proceeds must go into sports facilities. Although the proceeds from land sold to developers often goes to fund an indoor sports facility, many argue that this does not help sports like rugby which require an outdoor space.

School assemblies

By law, schools must have a 'daily act of collective worship' which should be 'wholly or mainly of a broadly Christian character'. The headteacher, in consultation with the governors, decides on the format and content of assemblies, and there is enough flexibility within the law to suit the needs and backgrounds of most pupils. If a headteacher feels that the religious and ethnic make-up of a school's pupils makes a 'broadly Christian' act of worship inappropriate, he can apply to the local Standing Advisory Council on Religious Education (SACRE) to have this requirement lifted. This is known as a 'determination'. SACREs are locally-appointed bodies which oversee the provision and quality of RE in each LEA and they report annually to the Qualifications and Curriculum Authority.

Parents who feel uncomfortable with the religious content of assemblies can apply for their child to be withdrawn from RE and assemblies. They do not have to give their reasons for this, but schools do have to comply. In practice only a small minority of children are withdrawn. In a culturally-mixed borough like Newham in East London, for example, only five children were exempted from having to attend assemblies.

Health problems

The Department of Education and Skills reckons that at any given time there are around 100,000 children and young people being educated outside school because of long-term injury or illness. The 1996 Education Act says that:

> Each local authority shall make arrangements for the provision of suitable education at school or otherwise for those children of compulsory school age who, by reason of illness, exclusion from school or otherwise may not for any period receive suitable education unless such arrangements are made for them.

DfES and the Department of Health guidelines set out the minimum standards that children who are ill or infirm can expect from the education system:

- LEAs should ensure that children are not at home without access to education for more than 15 working days.
- Children should receive a minimum of five hours teaching per week, although ideally they should get more than this, especially if public examinations are approaching.
- If a child develops some illness or injury that looks long term, plans for education should be made from day one.
- Children unable to attend school should have access to a broad and balanced curriculum.
- There should be close liaison between schools, health carers, parents and the LEA.
- Schools must have a policy for pupils unable to attend school for medical reasons and have a named member of staff responsible for it.
- The school should liaise with whoever is delivering the out-of-school education to inform them of the pupil's capabilities and programme of work.
- There should be somebody at the LEA responsible for pupils unable to attend school for medical reasons.
- Children should be reintegrated into their home school wherever possible and should be given educational support if this is a gradual process.

This education can take the form of home-teaching, a hospital teaching service (some hospitals have schools attached) or an integrated hospital/home education service.

In the case of regular or long-term absences, your child should have a Planned Education Programme to support the continuity of his education and to make sure he has access to as much education as his medical condition allows.

If your child needs regular medication while at school, the school and its staff are not responsible for administering it. While teachers and other school staff have a duty to act as any 'reasonably prudent parent' would to make sure pupils are healthy and safe on school premises (and on outings and trips), they are under no legal or contractual duty to administer or supervise the self-administration of medicines.

Administering medicines is something that staff do on a voluntary basis, and ideally they should be trained to do so. Very few schools have nurses these days. It is up to the headteacher of the school to decide if the school can help a pupil who needs medication. Most schools try to encourage self-administration by pupils of, for example, asthma inhalers or injections for diabetics. In many areas the NHS Trust has a School Health Service which advises pupils, parents and staff on these kinds of issues.

Children with medical needs have the same rights of admission to school as other children and cannot generally be excluded from school for medical reasons.

ELEVEN

Getting Ready for Secondary School

The uniform at my school is way too strict. You're not even allowed to have quiffs or highlights or anything. You have to have a set hairstyle. They won't let you have any sort of individuality. If you want to wear your hair like that then you should be allowed to.

Louis, 15

Just as primary school seemed a lifetime away as you pushed your baby in the pram, so secondary school seems a long way off as you try to decipher their first written words. Both things come around much sooner than you think, usually before we are ready for them.

How soon you start thinking about secondary schools will depend on where you live. In a rural area there may be no choice of schools and it is almost a non-issue while in London, which the Greater London Authority reckons needs another 25–30 secondary schools, parents are fretting about secondary league tables before their child has taken their first SATs.

There is a bewildering array of different types of secondary school to further confuse parents. They are basically divided into four groups depending on who runs admissions and who owns the buildings:

Community Schools – These are state comprehensives similar to the former county schools, under LEA ownership and control, where the LEA employ the staff and is the admissions authority.

Foundation Schools – The governing body is the employer and the admissions authority. The school's land and buildings are owned either by the governing body or a charitable foundation.

Voluntary-aided schools – Faith schools are voluntary aided schools. The governing body is the employer and the admissions authority. The school's land and buildings will be owned by a charitable foundation or, in the case of faith schools, by the church. The governing body contributes towards the capital costs of the school.

Voluntary-controlled schools – The LEA is the employer and the admissions authority. The school's land and buildings will normally be owned by a charitable foundation.

Within these groupings there are different types of schools:

Middle Schools – Some LEAs still operate a system of middle schools whereby children go to primary school until the age of nine, then they attend a middle school until they are 13 when they go to high school. The system is being phased out, partly because it does not sit comfortably with the Key Stages of the National Curriculum.

City academies – Academies were introduced in 2000 in disadvantaged areas to replace existing schools or to create more places where they are needed. They are all-ability schools established by sponsors from business, faith or voluntary groups. The sponsors provide about £2million towards the building costs and has a controlling interest in the governing body while the DfES pays for all the running costs. Fifty three academies – thirty of them in London – should be open by 2008.

Specialist Schools – The Specialist Schools programme was started in 1994 and the government sees it as key to raising standards in secondary education. It is only found in England where specialist schools represent nearly half of all secondary schools. Under the programme schools focus on one or two specialisms while providing a balanced education and delivering the National Curriculum. Schools with a specialism can select up to 10% of pupils on the basis of their aptitude for one or more specialist subjects. There are schools with specialisms in music, arts, humanities, science, engineering, languages, business and enterprise, maths and computing, sports and technology. The government would eventually like to see all schools become specialist schools.

City Technology Colleges – City Technology Colleges are independent all-ability schools for pupils aged 11–18. They are only found in urban areas in England and offer a wide range of vocational qualifications post-16. They usually have close links to business.

Grammar Schools – There are 162 remaining grammar schools in England. Scotland and Wales have never had grammar schools while in Northern Ireland there is a fully-selective grammar school system with admissions determined by the 11-plus. Some areas, like Kent and Buckinghamshire, have maintained the old grammar school system whereby all children sit a test to determine whether they will get into a grammar school. They are non fee-paying schools and entry is determined on academic ability alone. In other areas there may only be one school which has kept its grammar status and competition for places is usually very high.

Admissions

Secondary school admissions have been undergoing some changes in recent years as the old system was seen as chaotic and, in many cases, unfair. The concept of parental choice has come to mean that instead of parents choosing schools, schools seem to have their pick of the pupils. The temptation to choose the brightest, most motivated pupils from the most supportive backgrounds proved too much for many schools and covert and overt selection became common. This works to the disadvantage of children from poorer backgrounds where parents may not be so clued up or have the resources to work the system.

The 2002 Education Act brought some changes to the admissions procedure like the creation of admissions forums which were created to promote local discussion between all those bodies with an interest in admissions. In 2003 a new code of practice was introduced to create a fairer admissions procedure. All LEAs are to use the procedure from 2005 and, where possible, from 2004.

The aim of the code is to prevent the confusion under the old system where some children would receive multiple offers of places and others would not receive any. These offers came at different times so people held onto offers of places until they had heard from all the schools they had applied to.

The main points are:

- LEAs will coordinate admissions policy within the LEA and eventually there will be inter-LEA cooperation.

- There will be a common application form on which parents rank their three chosen schools both within and outside their LEA.

- All children will receive an offer of a secondary school place on March 1st.

- Interviewing parents or pupils is supposed to be banned but this is not statutory so may end up being tested in court.

- Children in care should be given a priority when schools choose intake.

The biggest change is that all children will receive one offer of a secondary school place on March 1st this applies to all maintained schools including faith schools or grammar schools. As is the case now, parents will have the right to an independent appeal panel if they are refused a place at a school.

Although this resolves the problem of receiving multiple offers of places and differing local timetables for admissions it does not solve the problem of how a school selects its pupils. A report by the London School of Economics found that covert and overt selection was alive and well in the secondary school system – especially among voluntary-aided and foundation schools. The report found that even City Technology Colleges, that are intended to represent the full ability range in the catchment area, used devices like school reports, 'aptitude' tests, writing tests to assess 'motivation' and questions relating to parents' occupations.

This kind of selection obviously has an impact on the other secondary schools in the area. If the brightest pupils have been creamed off by the popular schools (who are also likely to score low on inclusiveness) then the other schools are left to cope with higher levels of social problems and disadvantage.

Selection

No maintained primary school is selective but at secondary level, as we have seen, there is some selection. This takes one of the following forms:

Former Grant-Maintained Schools – Under the Conservative government in the late 1980s schools were allowed to 'opt out' of council control and take over the running of their budgets. Under this system these 'grant-maintained' schools became partially selective and were allowed to select a proportion of their pupils by whatever criteria they liked.

When the Labour Government was elected in 1997 they said there would be no new selection but that schools that already selected would be allowed to continue to do so. They introduced a rather complicated process whereby local parents could initiate a ballot to decide whether to keep selection in a particular school. This has only been used once, unsuccessfully, in Ripon. Attempts in recent years by the schools adjudicator to reduce the level of selection in some schools have been overturned in the High Court. The adjudicator's role is to consider objections from parents and also from one school about another's admission procedure and it can rule out or modify these procedures (except those with a statutory basis).

Banding – In order to ensure a mixed ability intake some secondaries practice 'banding'. Children applying to the school may sit a test or their SATs results will be used to put them in a band. If there are more children in one band than there are places at the school the school should allocate places according to their normal oversubscription criteria.

Grammar Schools – Wholly selective on ability alone.

Specialist Schools – Can select up to 10% of pupils on the basis of their aptitude in the relevant specialism.

Who chooses?

The process of deciding which secondary school is right for your child is basically the same as with primary school – a mixture of research, rumour and gut reaction. Have a look at Chapter 3 for advice on how to approach it. The big difference this time is that your child will expect to have a say.

Arguments in favour of children choosing:

- They are the ones going to the school. If they have played a part in choosing it they are likely to be more committed.
- You have probably brought them up to express their views so it would be unfair not to expect them to have a say in this decision.
- If you choose a school they don't like they could perform badly through unhappiness or resentment.

Arguments against children choosing:

- They will probably want to go where all their friends are going regardless of whether it is right for them.
- It is too big a burden to put on a 10-year-old.
- If it all goes wrong at least they will have someone to blame.

In the end it is probably best to give consideration to their views but not for that to be the only factor. Try to talk through their reasons for wanting to go to a particular school and really discuss with them whether they are valid reasons. If your choice is unpopular are there any older pupils you know there who will soften your child's opposition to the school in question? Examine the reasons why you oppose their first choice. Are they important enough to risk your child developing an anti-school attitude?

Single sex or mixed?

While most primaries are mixed, secondary schools are often single sex, especially if they are faith or grammar schools. Most people have pretty strong views on whether they want their child to go to a single-sex or mixed school and that usually depends on which type of school they went to and what their experience of it was.

In general, research seems to show that academically, girls do better in a single-sex environment while boys do better in a mixed environment. In practice it is probably best to look at the school rather than be hung-up on its hormonal content. Here are some points to consider:

- If you are looking at a single-sex school does your child have other opportunities to mix with members of the opposite sex?
- If it is a mixed school, what is the level of pastoral care? Is the Personal Social and Health Education and Citizenship part of the national curriculum central to its approach?
- In either case are there male and female members of staff to provide strong role models?

Starting secondary school

It was the most difficult thing that I've ever had to deal with and that she's had to deal with. It was constant. The whole thing about learning how to get to school on your own – she'd always been with me. On Monday morning she had to remember to buy her bus pass. She always has to carry her bus pass or remember to bring books from home. I can't run up to school and give them to her. So there was all of that – remembering the PE kit or remembering her musical instruments on the right days, and remembering to give me letters. The schools are so much bigger so that whole thing of moving around classrooms and remembering your way to different classrooms and remembering your books because you're not allowed back in your class once the lesson has started, so if you've left your books in your locker or desk you are done for.

Rebecca, mother of Rachel 13, Matthew 11, Thomas, 9 and Esther, 6.

Starting secondary school is a big deal. It is still school but not as primary school children know it. They are much bigger places and for a child to familiarize themselves with all the nooks and crannies can take weeks. Their populations are much bigger – and older. Even finding your friends in the playground can be a daunting experience when the playground is full of 16-year-olds. Children who have come from being the oldest in a primary school with accompanying responsibilities and status suddenly find themselves a small fish in a big pond. The anonymity and lack of recognition of past successes can be very demoralizing for an 11-year-old.

The level of pastoral care is generally strong in primary schools while at secondary they are sometimes thrown in at the deep end. There is nobody checking they have had lunch and they are not cut much slack if they forget books, gym kits, homework after the first week or so.

> With my older one recently starting in secondary school it's quite a change and a learning experience for me. They use diaries there so if I need to communicate with the teachers I guess I could write something in there like 'could you please explain the homework to her' but it feels so formal I don't really like that. It's not like primary school. It would be nice to be more involved at secondary school but I guess it's different. The teachers have to make the children achieve certain things for their league tables to look good so they are pressured and don't really have the time. So it's going to be difficult. It's all new, maybe next year I'll feel different.
>
> Sharmaine, mother of Denika 12 and Kiana, 9.

As a parent you may find it hard to adjust to the change in the parent-school relationship. Instead of dealing with one class teacher your child will have a form teacher and then different teachers for all the subjects in the curriculum. At primary you were welcomed into the classroom and invited on school trips – most secondary schools stick to the rather old-fashioned view that a parent's place is outside the school gate. The government is trying to change this situation as it realizes the educational benefits of parental involvement are important at secondary level just as at primary, but don't expect as much communication from the school.

The rather brutal nature of the primary-secondary transfer does have an impact on children's schooling. Research undertaken over the last 20 years has shown that students' work falls off when they start secondary school with about 2 out of 5 failing to make any progress on standardized tests in English, maths and reading by the end of their first year. More days are taken off sick during year 7 than at any other time. What kind of start they make to secondary school can impact on their whole school career especially when they are streamed.

> At secondary school you are more independent. If you don't take care of what you do then you are punished so you have to depend on yourself to do stuff.
>
> Say you don't do your homework, your homework is not up to standard, or you've been chatting in class you will get 'academics'. An 'academic' is when you have to bring a piece of work into the hall and you have to do it there – an essay to write or something. There is also a 'pastoral' which is for if you are late or been rude to a teacher or stuff like that. You have to go in the hall. It depends what year you are in how long you have to be in there.
>
> There's a category system – there's category 1, 2, 3 and 4. It depends how severe it is. If it's not that bad you get category 1 and they will call your parents. If it's category 2 the parents have to see your head of year. If it's category 3 you have to get reviewed by the headteacher and category 4 you get reviewed by the headteacher and excluded.
>
> Denika, 12.

Some educationalists claim that this fall off in performance is only relative to the intensive academic coaching children have been subjected to in Year 6 when they take their SATs but schools and LEAs are looking at strategies to soften the impact of the move. These include:

- Primary schools introducing specialist teaching in the last year to mimic secondary schools.
- Tighter deadlines to homework at the end of primary school.
- Some secondaries organize 'taster' sessions where pupils attend a day of half day at their likely secondary school.
- Older 'buddies' to act as mentors for new pupils.

- Bridging projects in some subjects to carry over from primary into secondary school.
- Increasing feedback to pupils at the beginning of secondary school as primary pupils are used to a more intimate relationship with their teachers.

I was anxious about leaving primary school as I didn't want to leave my friends behind as they were going to a different school to me. So I was sad about that but I did want to go on to the new school as it had a lab and I wanted to go and try new experiments and things. It's more stressful in the bigger schools because there are more people there and it's quite hard to make friends because you are in a new school and everyone else is making friends. Finding somebody in such a large school that you can actually be friends with is quite hard.

Justin, 11.

There are also things that you can do to help support them as they find their feet in a new school with a different regime:

- Take up opportunities to visit the new school whether it be for specially arranged open days, fairs or car boot sales.
- Make sure they are getting enough sleep.
- Expect their behaviour to regress a bit as they will probably feel a bit insecure at first.
- Help them create a system for remembering what they need to whether it is a weekly schedule stuck up on the fridge or a checklist on the front door.
- If they are involved in an extra-curricular activity keep it up so that school is not their whole existence.
- Settling in can take a while. Carefully observe them during the first term and talk to them about how they are finding new subjects, teachers and friendships.
- Take an interest in their homework but try not to interfere too much. They have to learn how to organize it themselves.
- Try not to pass on any anxiety you may have as they will soon pick up on this.

- Make sure they have all the kit they need so they don't feel at a disadvantage.
- Remind them that it is the same for all new children there. Everybody will be finding it a bit scary.

Finally, remember that secondary school, scary and anonymous as it can seem at first, can still be fun. Although there are not so many opportunities for parental involvement it is worth making the effort to meet other parents and involve yourself. Just as you did when your child started primary school.

RESOURCES

The Advisory Centre for Education (ACE)
www.ace-ed.org.uk
An independent advice centre for parents.
Exclusion Line: 020 7704 9822
General Advice Line: 0808 800 5793

The National Attention Deficit Disorder Information and Support Service
www.aldiss.co.uk
Tel: 020 8906 9068

Qualifications, Curriculum and Assessment Authority for Wales
www.accac.org.uk
Tel: 029 2037 5400

The National Autistic Society
www.nas.org.uk
Charity and campaigning organization for people with autistic spectrum disorders and their families.

The Scottish Society for Autism
www.autism-in-scotland.org.uk

The Basic Skills Agency
www.basic-skills.co.uk
Tel: 020 7405 4017

BBC websites
www.bbc.co.uk/schools

Learning resources for home and school.

www.bbc.co.uk/wales/schoolgate
Information for parents about schools and the education system in Wales.

The Book Trust
www.booktrust.org.uk
An independent educational charity to encourage lifelong reading.
Information helpline: 0906 516 1193

Bullying Online
www.bullying.co.uk
Help and advice for victims of bullying, their parents and their school.

The Anti-Bullying Campaign
Trained counsellors on hand to give support and advice.
Tel: 020 7378 1446

Childline
www.childline.org.uk
24-hour helpline for children in distress or danger.
Tel: 0800 1111

The Daycare Trust
www.daycaretrust.org.uk
Hotline providing free information and advice to parents.
Tel: 020 7840 3350

British Dyslexia Association
www.bda-dyslexia.org.uk
Tel: 0118 966 2677
Helpline: 0118 966 8271

Department of Education and Skills
www.dfes.gov.uk
www.dfes.gov.uk/leagateway
Information and services for LEAs from DfES and related bodies.

The Down's Syndrome Association
www.downs-syndrome.org.uk
Tel: 020 8682 4001

The Dyspraxia Foundation
www.dyspraxiafoundation.org.uk
Resource for parents and teenagers and adults with the condition. Runs local support groups.
8, West Alley, Hitchin, Hertfordshire, SG5 IEG

ESTYN – Chief Inspector of Education and Training in Wales
www.estyn.gov.uk
Tel: 029 2044 6446

Local Education Authorities
www.lea.org.uk

National Council of Parent Teacher Associations
www.ncpta.org.uk/

National Curriculum Online
www.nc.net.uk
The site links every National Curriculum programme of study requirement to resources online.

National Family and Parenting Institute
www.nfpi.org
An independent charity working to support parents in bringing up their children, to promote the wellbeing of families and to make society more family-friendly.
Tel: 020 7424 3460

The National Literacy Trust
www.literacytrust.org.uk
An independent charity dedicated to building a literate nation.

NSPCC
Free national helpline for anyone concerned about a child at risk of ill treatment or abuse.
Tel: 0800 800 5000

Ofsted

www.ofsted.gov.uk
For finding inspection reports on schools, LEAs and childcare providers.
Tel: 020 7421 6800

Parents in Wales

www.nfpi.org/parentsinwales

Parentline Plus

A free national helpline for parents.
Tel: 0808 800 2222

The Parent Centre

www.parentcentre.gov.uk
Government site giving information about education in the UK including curriculum, admissions and choosing a school.

Parentalk

www.parentalk.co.uk
A charity dedicated to inspiring and equipping parents to make the most of every stage of their child's growing up.

Parents 4 Schools

www.parents4schools.co.uk
Practical help for parents volunteering in schools.

Parents Online

www.parents.org.uk
Website to help parents with children at primary school.

Pre-school Learning Alliance

www.pre-school.org.uk
Head office: 020 7620 0550

Scottish Education

www.scotland.gov.uk
First stop for information on education in Scotland.
Tel: 0131 244 0911

www.LTScotland.org.uk
Public body providing support, resources and staff development for early years and school education in Scotland.
Tel: 08700 100 297

The National Association for Special Educational Needs
www.nasen.org.uk
Provides links to other organizations.
Tel: 01827 311 500

SEN
www.dfes.gov.uk/sen
Government centre for Special Educational Needs.

Schoolzone
www.schoolzone.co.uk
Educational search engine with advice and links for parents, teachers and students.

Tigerchild
www.tigerchild.com
Site for parents with links to other sites and information on a range of issues including education.

Index

admissions appeals – 22, 23
admissions bodies – 20, 24
Advanced Skills Teacher – 103
Adventure Activities Licensing
    Authority – 134
appeals panels – 23
applications – 20
Art and Design – 54
Asberger's syndrome – 120
assemblies – 138
attendance – 129–30
Attention Deficiency Disorder – 121
Attention Deficit Hyperactivity
    Disorder – 121
Autism – 120

Behavioural and Educational
    Support Teams – 122
behavioural problems – 111
bullying – 38, 91–6, 125

Callaghan, James – 42
catchment area – 15
changing schools – 24
childminders – 133
circle time – 108–9
citizenship – 55–6
city technology colleges – 6
class sizes – 23
classroom assistants – 105–106

Department of Education and Skills
    – 3, 16, 76, 128
Design and Technology – 54
discipline – 89–91
Down's Syndrome – 121
Dyslexia – 119–20
Dyspraxia – 123

early years centre – 2
Education Act 1993 – 112
Education Act 1981 – 111
Education Act 1944 – 1, 111
Education Reform Act 1988 – 3, 13

educational psychologist – 106, 122
educational welfare officer – 106
emotional and behavioural
    difficulties – 122
English – 51
Equal Opportunities cCommission –
    129
Excellence in Cities scheme – 124
exclusions – 24, 130–32
extended schools – 31

faith schools – 7, 21
Foundation Stage – 11, 43
Foundation Stage Profile – 44
friendship – 83–6
friendship stop – 84–5

gender differences – 69–70
General Teaching Council – 104
Geography – 54
gifted children – 124–5
governing body – 37

health problems – 139–40
History – 54
home-school agreements – 38, 127
homework – 73–8, 123–4
homework clubs – 74–5

inclusion – 111–113
independent schools – 8
Individual Education Plans –
    114–116
individual learning styles – 60
Induction – 25, 30
Information and Communication
    Technology – 54
initial teaching alphabet – 61–2
INSET days – 107
Institute of Education – 48
intervention programmes – 68–9

Key Stages – 3, 44

league tables – 13, 16, 18–19, 48
learning mentors – 106
learning through play – 12
learning to read – 61–5
learning to write – 65–7
literacy hour – 63
Local Education Authorities – 4, 16, 21, 69, 112, 117
London School of Economics – 59
Local Government Association – 6

Maths – 53, 67
middle schools – 3
multiple intelligences – 111
Music – 54

National Childcare Strategy – 9
national curriculum – 43–58
National Literacy Strategy – 62
National Numeracy Strategy – 62
National Primary Strategy – 44, 50
neighbourhood nurseries initiative – 11
Northern Ireland – 5, 50
Numeracy Hour – 63

Ofsted – 4
Ofsted report – 17

parental choice – 14
parent governors – 36
parent governor representatives – 37
Parent-Teacher Association – 18, 35
parents evenings – 34
peer pressure – 86–7
phonics – 62
physical disabilities – 119
Physical Education – 55, 137–8
positive reinforcement – 108
PSHE – 55–7, 98
Pupil Referral Units – 133

Qualification and Curriculum Authority – 5, 138

Qualified Teacher Status – 100

reception class – 26
reflective listening – 80–81
Religious Education – 55, 138

SATs – 47, 96
school councils – 90
school dinners – 136–7
school refusal – 81
school terms – 6
school trips – 134–5
Science – 54
Scotland – 5, 49
self-esteem – 87–9
Sex and Relationship Education – 57
smacking – 132
Special Eductional Needs – 16
Special Educational Needs and Disability Act 2002 – 112, 119
Special Educational Needs Co-ordinator – 106, 114
Special Needs Register – 114
starting school – 25
statements – 111, 116–117
stress – 49, 96
Subject Coordinator – 106
summer babies – 72–3
supplementary schools – 70–71
Sure Start – 11

teacher training – 99
Teacher Training Agency – 5
teachers – 99
transport – 124
truancy – 129–30

uniform – 26, 128–9

vetting of teachers – 101

Wales – 5, 49